IS THEOLOGY A SCIENCE?

IS VOLUME

2

OF THE

Twentieth Century Encyclopedia of Catholicism

UNDER SECTION

I

KNOWLEDGE AND FAITH

IT IS ALSO THE

23RD

VOLUME IN ORDER OF PUBLICATION

Edited by HENRI DANIEL-ROPS of the Académie Française

IS THEOLOGY A SCIENCE?

By M. D. CHENU, O.P.

Translated from the French by A. H. N. GREEN-ARMYTAGE

HAWTHORN BOOKS · PUBLISHERS · *New York*

First Edition, August, 1959

NIHIL OBSTAT

Johannes M. T. Barton, S.T.D., L.S.S.

Censor Deputatus

IMPRIMATUR

E. Morrogh Bernard

Vicarius Generalis

Westmonasterii, die VI MARTII MCMLIX

CONTENTS

INTRODUCTION

It may occasion some surprise that one of the opening volumes of this series, whose object is to present both the subject-matter and the history of the Christian faith to the general public, should start with the question, "Is theology a science?" Surely this is a very technical, even academic, problem, best suited for discussion by theologians in their professional debates. Simple church-goers like ourselves have neither the ability nor the inclination to engage in such esoteric controversies, and might not our simple faith be overburdened by the weight of so much rationalistic curiosity? May we not, in fact, contaminate the revealed Word of God by bringing into our world of warm and lowly adoration those ideas and methods which rational science, so-called, has developed for its own ends? The very simplicity of the Gospel is surely the hall-mark of its divine transcendence.

That is precisely the question. And today it is not a question merely for teachers and specialists. An answer to it is demanded by the faithful at large, and this appetite of theirs— no idle or academic curiosity but a vital and spontaneous quest—is a sign of health. Indeed, there is at this juncture no more valuable proof of the spiritual stability of the Christian people than this appetite for theological education—as was shown, to take one example among many, by the publication and success of *Theology Library*[1] by A. M. Henry, O.P. The biblical and liturgical movements, missionary zeal and pastoral enthusiasm—all these are Christian awakenings of the first importance; but it might have happened that in their fervent attachment to their own chief objects these movements might have become shut in upon themselves. This would have en-

[1] Four volumes, translated from the French (Chicago, Fides Publishers, 1955–7).

tailed a lack of balance—if not in individuals at least in the community of the Church. It is an excellent thing that there has developed within them, and without in any way diverting them from their proper goals, this organic curiosity concerning the faith—a curiosity which it is the duty and privilege of the theologians to satisfy.

"What I believe is what my parish priest teaches." Time was when such a rule of faith could be proclaimed with some complacency and with a touch of humorous bravado which even the genius of a Paul Claudel might voluntarily adopt; and when spoken in a truly simple faith and childlike obedience the words do have a certain value. But unless we are on our guard this simple faith may become the faith of a simpleton, this reverence for authority may turn to clericalism and this childlike submission to childishness. "The faith of a charcoal-burner" may be all very well for charcoal-burners—charcoal-burners of past centuries. It will be of little use to the man of 1950, faced by a world where he must be an adult, not merely in order to earn his living but also in order to believe. An adult faith arms itself with theology, for an inward understanding of the Word of God is the fairest homage which a human being can render to the God who speaks to him.

In reading the Gospel we may be subconsciously seduced, by the very charm of its simplicity, into an ill-judged narrow-mindedness, not appreciating the true humanity of that dialogue which God does really hold with mankind—starting with Abraham, father of all believers, and finding its supreme realization in Christ, God's incarnate Son. The incarnation of that Word follows its own course in my spirit; my spirit, by the light of faith, pronounces the Word of God. The shock which that Word, that infinitely unmerited grace, produces in me is not thereby deadened. On the contrary, it seizes upon all the fibres of my mind and inspires me to build up within myself and into the whole rational fabric of my understanding, the elements of that same Word. Assuredly this travail must have its laws, laws which cannot be confined within the language of what is usually known as science, and the promulgation of these laws is the task which now lies before us. But to start with we must test the religious validity of such a task, at various levels.

At one of these levels we meet the technical question of a "theological science", a question which forms part of the understanding of our faith. But it is the purpose of this series to go beyond that special sector of theology wherein the professionals organize, systematize and elaborate their premises and conclusions. All such technical work belongs to the inner regions of a more extensive field of study (ranging from the reading of Scripture to the moral actions of individuals) wherein all the manifold resources of the mind are set to work at understanding the content of revealed truth in the light of faith. Thus St Thomas, following the Fathers, gave to the word "theology" (literally "sacred teaching") its whole meaning without detracting from its more formally scientific functions.

This, then, is the position we propose to adopt and this the scope we propose to embrace in answering the question posed on the title-page; and thus do we hope to satisfy, to the best of our ability, the appetite of contemporary Christians who desire in all good faith to "do theology".

CHAPTER I

THE PROBLEM

Theology a *science*? First we must resolve the ambiguity, the rather crude ambiguity, which obscures that word. We are not here concerned with science—its objects, methods and constitution—as the term is commonly understood in the generally accepted vocabulary of today. No question but that the foremost characteristic of the civilization which we call modern is the development of a form of knowledge which, operating on the far side of perception but on the hither side of philosophy, organically analyses the phenomena of nature to discover their laws and, by discerning relationships between facts and laws, proceeds to increasingly general hypotheses. This process which we so much admire had its origin, so far as the west is concerned, in the empirical and philosophical inquiries of the ancient Greeks. It was they who first wrote the foundation-charter of our knowledge of man and of the world, and the subsequent history and progress of science give the lie to those Positivists who have sought to exalt the experimental and practical functions of science at the expense of reason—by whose power alone the synthesis is achieved.

Science, without trespassing on the preserves of philosophy, has at all times established itself on that level of intelligibility which its methods, laws and (in the words of Meyerson) its "natural ontology" demand. Hence comes, with a passion that is sometimes undisciplined but also with a genuine grandeur, the so-called "scientific spirit"—testing every statement by experiment, according objective validity only to such knowledge as has been so worked out and tested, criticizing all results by tried and proved methods of demonstration and verification, and finally, at its most profound, proclaiming the intelligibility of the real world through a rational study of its relations and laws—such are the basic assumptions of the scientific spirit, even if they are sometimes held unconsciously. Reason and experiment are thus the two mainsprings of science.

Now it is clearly impossible to treat the subject-matter of theology—always assuming that God can be an object of human knowledge at all—along the lines and according to the methods of "science" as defined above. The very nature of science rules it out. If knowledge is conditioned by the nature of its object it is obvious that a knowledge of divinity, and especially of a God who reveals himself to man in all his mystery, is something incommensurable with any knowledge of natural phenomena. And conversely, as history shows, anyone who takes this science as his sole pattern for the life of the mind will be drawn inevitably towards a denial of God.

But if human reason be not confined to the phenomena of nature alone, if it be capable of attaining to the supreme cause which underlies their appearances, if at the root of their being it discerns the necessity for a source of all being, then, whatever name we choose to employ for it, there exists in the field of human understanding an area which is "superscientific". It will, of course, have laws and methods of its own but it will be truth—truth to be discovered and rationally rebuilt within my mind. Moreover, if this source of being is found to be a person, a living person, a person, indeed, whose love has created, as if by emanation, another being fashioned in his likeness and with whom he can enter into a communion of knowledge and love, then I am faced with an unfathomable mystery—a mystery whose claims upon my faith ought assuredly to be scrutinized but a mystery, too, which it must be a delight to understand. This will also be a sort of knowledge but a very special and original sort whose object far transcends the scope of natural reason. The mystery of God can only be reached in faith. I "believe" what he has revealed about himself, and this means taking part in a life whose very first act is to accept the word he speaks to me.

Faith, not science. The opposition of these terms is fashionable—and valid, too, if science be understood in the sense described above. On this level science and faith cannot co-exist. It would be impossible to pass from one to the other. But what we have in mind is not any tyrannizing of one over the other—as would happen if either science or theology arrogated to itself totalitarian authority—but a natural application, on two different levels, to disparate objectives. I can deny the existence of God, or deny his revelation, but if he does exist, if he has revealed himself, then my knowledge of him will not be "scientific" in the sense defined above.

The incompatible character of these two ways or modes of knowledge is established by simple observation. Belief, having for its object a mystery—the mystery of a creator-God and, moreover, a self-revealing God—is a knowledge defined and qualified by its relationship to the supreme Being. Encounter with that Being and penetration into it are holy things. Religion differs in kind and in texture from science and even from metaphysics. It emanates from my own being—in an act of understanding, no doubt, but also in an "engagement" (as the modern phrase has it) which grapples with me in the very source of my life and destiny. It implies a gift, more or less consciously accepted, in which are mingled a reverent awe in the face of the grandeur of that Being, a sense that my happiness can only be accomplished in him, and a conviction that he is the sole Absolute in whom all values have their foundation. As compared with science, in fact, belief—and especially the Christian faith—involves an *inwardness* which is equally averse to the objectivity and cold rationality which, as we have said, are the indispensable conditions for a critical investigation of nature.

How then in this belief, this sacred knowledge, this divine revelation, can we envisage the possibility of a science?

OPPOSITION TO A THEOLOGICAL SCIENCE

A Christian, in fact, is convinced of this incompatibility in direct proportion to the simplicity of his faith. His loyalty and his trust alike persuade him spontaneously to reject the introduction of rational processes of investigation into this sphere. He is content before the Father of heaven to look upward like a little child, as the Gospel counsels. At his first encounter with Christ he was, indeed, able to demand what were Christ's credentials for making that startling claim to incarnate Godhead; but once he has accepted Christ's love he simply "follows" him. He debates no longer. He hearkens. He submits to the testimony of the Holy Spirit.

Many people therefore regard theology—a systematic knowledge, cross-braced by reasons—as a tiresome concession to that spirit of curiosity which is the temptation, gravely misplaced in this instance, lying in wait for Reason. Perhaps I may meet with some "reasons" in the mystery, some proportions and harmonies in the divine encounter, but in so far as I attach myself to such reasons my faith will be imperilled. It will no longer be a pure, simple-hearted attachment of love. Reason, in short, is impertinent—in every sense of the word.

Why, the very theologians themselves, these believers turned professors, proclaim how impertinent it is. What is there in common between the simplicity of the Gospel and the complexity of a *Summa Theologica*? Between the unfathomable mystery and these vague conclusions drawn from syllogisms? Between the brotherhood of the faith and this private world of initiates where disputation erodes the substance of communion? This "science" of the faith can be nothing but an eccentricity, certainly tedious and possibly dangerous. Let us leave the theologians where they belong, in the schools.

This is a case that has often been brought to trial before now. It crops up periodically among Christians—either in this radical form or in the more polite opposition between "mystical" and "speculative" theology. Without quite going to these extremes the masters of the spiritual life do distinguish two different "ways" within the boundaries of the most earnest faith. Thus St Bonaventure has distinguished among the saints those who, like the Seraphim, delivered themselves up to be dissolved in love (and this was the way of his own master St Francis) and those who, like the Cherubim, devoted themselves to the pursuit of knowledge (such as his friend the Dominican Thomas Aquinas). Moreover the theologians, when placed in the witness-box, do not always agree. Many of them, and not the least considerable, have refused to grant theology the character of a science—or have granted it only after such qualifications as greatly reduce its applicability.

The problem, therefore, involves a whole range of questions, rising tier upon tier from a basis in undisputed essentials right up to optional opinions where the Church, indeed, has left us free to choose but where solid convictions may nevertheless be attained. We must therefore expect an analysis where the very possibility of certitude depends upon the subtlest nuances.

UNWITTING THEOLOGIANS

So you are not interested in taking up theology? But you have already taken it up, without knowing it. Yes, you especially, the devout believer with the simple evangelical faith. You have just been taking part in a eucharistic service where the altar of sacrifice was turned towards the people. After a momentary surprise at this innovation (though it is founded on tradition) you understand the reason for the change, and the very expression "taking part" which you now use instead of the phrase "going to Mass" bespeaks an *understanding* of the sacred mystery which goes further than a mere renewal of fervour. In this understanding of the faith you are practising theology.

You have just read the Song of Songs, that wonderful little book about the marriage of God and humanity. The realism of the language did not embarrass you because you understood that in this sacred book it is normal to express truths about the ways of God in the most earth-bound images; and so you interpreted the text by the rules of that literary genre which, in parables, expresses a comparison not by a detailed allegory but by a general play of metaphor. In this critical interpretation of the word of God you were practising theology.

In reading the works of St Teresa you find not only material for devout contemplation but a conception of union with God, of the practice of virtue and of progress in grace to which you can wholeheartedly assent; whereas you find Rodriguez's *Practice of Perfection* neither attractive nor useful to you. You do not, of course, go so far as to question the orthodoxy of either of these different forms of spirituality, since both are approved by the Church, but you opt for St Teresa, experimentally and doctrinally. You are, so to speak, of her school. In so choosing you are making a theological decision.

You belong to a Catholic Action group and your attitude is moulded by a particular view of what constitutes salvation—a view derived not merely from missionary zeal but from a characteristic perception of what constitutes a state of grace in Christ. You have rediscovered the mystery of the Incarnation and in your meditation you dwell on the humanity of Christ in the unity of the divine essence. You delight to nourish your faith in the mystical body of Christ. And you are practising theology—without knowing anything of the ancient controversies about the Incarnation nor of how the Fathers of Antioch championed the humanity of Christ whereas the Alexandrians preferred to contemplate the unity of the Word. You have (unconsciously but profoundly) followed one current of theological thought which, although always approved by the Church, assesses the complex gifts of the mystery of the Incarnation in a manner different from another.

You are concerned with the problem of Christianity in the world. You want to bear testimony on the side of justice and brotherly love. You are faced with the social situation and the appropriation of material goods by individuals. It is a system

which has its roots in human nature, no doubt, but it quickly
degenerates into an odious excess, and is now brought to the
bar by a new form of society which claims that the distribution
of wealth can only be made, in justice and charity, by the intervention of the established powers that be, official or political.
So you find yourself forced to reflect on the justification for
private property as such. Do you consider it a means whereby
each person is assured of economic living-space? Or do you
regard it as the least inefficient way of distributing the wealth
of the community for the common good? In your decision you
will be making a theological judgement, and indeed choosing
between two theological theories of property.

A press campaign about oil discoveries in the Sahara is in
full swing. The public, gloomily contemplating the economic
outlook in France, rushes eagerly towards this new dawn of
hope. Nearly five millions are subscribed in one day. One
company makes a capital issue of forty millions, and so on.
The poverty-stricken Treasury plans to sell its rights in all this
land to private interests, to "de-nationalize" the oil-prospect-
ing undertakings. Should a Christian deputy vote, against the
Socialists, for the bill which surrenders control of so much
wealth to powerful groups of financiers? What says moral
theology? The casuists of old had only a primitive economy
to deal with—the small-town market and the usury of petty
bankers. They could not foresee the world-economy of today.
But have they no message for us? No light to throw on our
problems?

You are engaged in problems of labour organization, you
are concerned for the political and economic emancipation of
the under-developed peoples, perplexed by the ambiguity of
nationalism, responsible in part (and willynilly) for the worldly
needs and aspirations of non-Christians, aware that atheists
have made real contributions in the field of earthly values; you
hesitate about which challenges to accept, which institutions
to support, conscious that a Christian is inevitably set apart
from the world yet at the same time convinced that you are the

leaven in the lump, by virtue of the Gospel. What should you do? What principle should you follow? What practical decisions should you take? Hear the words of Pius XII himself, giving in a discourse a lesson in theology which contains both magisterial teaching and a theological analysis of the human predicament in a progressing world—a theology, we might say, of Nature and Grace:

> Does this mean that we cannot, for the service of the community, collaborate with institutions which do not expressly recognize God as the author and legislator of the universe? [He is alluding to the cultural and educative programme of Unesco for the underdeveloped countries, which some people had refused to support because of its religious neutrality.] It is important, here, to distinguish different levels of cooperation. In fact, without forgetting that his ultimate aim is to contribute to the eternal salvation of his brethren, the Christian will remind himself that the coming of the kingdom of God into the hearts and social institutions of men requires some minimum of human encouragement, an appeal to simple reason, to which all men normally submit even if they have not the grace of the faith. . . . Therefore, the Christian will be ready to work for the relief of all material misery and the development everywhere of elementary education; in a word, for any enterprise having in view the amelioration of the lot of the poor and the disinherited. In so doing he is certainly fulfilling a duty of collective charity in preparing to bring a greater number of people into a personal life worthy to be so called. . . . For reason alone suffices to establish the basic rights of peoples. . . . It is therefore desirable that Catholics should cooperate in all institutions which, in theory and practice, respect the principles of natural law.[1]

Your devotion to the Blessed Virgin appears to you, and rightly, as a test of the genuineness of your faith in the plan of the Incarnation. You wish to establish this faith, emotional as it is, on a firm footing, the better to understand both the graces and the privileges of our Lady. And you understand—without ever having thought it out in theory but merely in order to

[1] Allocution to the Assembly of *Pax Romana*, April 1957.

build up your faith—that the summit of those graces and the full measure of those privileges is to be found in the divine motherhood of Mary. Thus do you profit by theology which, in recent decades, has made great and happy progress in its teaching about the Blessed Virgin.

And so on. The instances might be extended indefinitely. You may not attend a theological college, and doubtless you do not need to—although the existence of such colleges, re-member, may be necessary for an organized knowledge of the faith in a Church which is faith's sacred depositary. But you are practising theology (just as Molière's hero was talking prose) without knowing it. It would be better if you did know it. It is by knowing what he is about that a man becomes adult. So with the Christian. An adult is one who, taking cognizance of what he possesses, reflects thereon, analyses it, builds up its resources, unifies it. The theologian is an adult Christian who, taking cognizance of what he possesses, reflects upon it, analyses the complex content of his faith, builds it up, unifies it.

OBJECTIONS

We have no wish to minimize the objections nor disguise the limits to this inquiry—or rather, to misconstrue the psycho-logical, epistemological and spiritual conditions of such a rational activity within the faith. To ponder my faith, to con-strue within myself the word of God, to incarnate his light within the fabric of my mind—it is a fair hazard, as Plato said of the contemplation of God.

The first objection is the one posed by St Thomas himself, the man who, in spite of criticism, explicitly accorded to theology the character of a science. The mysteries of God, both in his own existence and in his plans, are inaccessible to us without the infused light of faith; to introduce into that light a rational process, by its nature incongruous, will at the very least disturb our free communion with God and, in the words of St Thomas's adversary St Bonaventure, dilute the wine of the knowledge of God with the water of human reasoning.

In fact (the objector goes on) there is no common denominator between the diverse operations of science—analyses, definitions, proofs—and the transcendent mystery. God, "an unbounded ocean of infinite reality", as St John Damascene beautifully expressed it in the seventh century, can obviously not be confined within a definition framed in terms of "proximate genus" and "specific differentia". His freely-made decisions in the business of our salvation—the Incarnation of his Son, the manner of preaching the Gospel, the passion, death and resurrection of Christ, the descent of the Holy Spirit, the foundation of the Church and so forth, including such major "episodes" as the bodily assumption of Mary—these cannot be submitted to a demonstration whose validity rests upon necessary connections between the nature and properties of objects. The analyses, distinctions and divisions whereby our mental concepts develop have no point of contact with his divine unity, and our modes of speech cannot be applied to him without profound modification. At bottom, in all these operations, it is the desire for what is rational and the search for evidence—those two essential components of the scientific spirit—which are checkmated when faced by the visible or invisible epiphany of God.

Furthermore, when we examine the theologian's modes of reasoning we find that he himself avoids any such misplaced rigour. He deals in similitudes, not forgetting their inadequacy and indefiniteness. Men have always dreamed of confining the beauties of form and harmony within mathematical equations, but even Plato, mathematician as he was, had recourse to myths when speaking of the "Form of the Good" and its creative emanations. So let us leave science to its proper subject-matter and keep faith for God.

Besides, it is not merely the techniques of science which come into play; its content, too, will creep surreptitiously into the domain of faith. For example, in order to analyse the work-

ings of grace we must accept some definition of human nature;
when describing the mechanism of faith we must presuppose
a theory of human understanding; in order to define creation
we must adopt a particular view of the world and its evolution.
In this way the revelation of God will be most incongruously
invaded by unexpected and quite earthly factors, according as
my philosophy happens to offer such and such a conception of
causality, such and such a psychology of liberty, such and such
a theory of the union of body and soul, such and such a definition of happiness, such and such a view of human society. And
theology does in fact branch out into theological "systems"
differing from one another not in respect of their orthodoxy
but in their philosophical bases. And the theologians agree that
these systems, as such, are to be distinguished not by reference
to faith, orthodoxy or religion, but simply by their scientific
value. Well, they give scope for controversy among professionals, perhaps, but throw no supernatural light upon the road
to the Beatific Vision. Experience shows how dogmatically
relative they are as a result of the varying philosophic attitudes
which they presuppose. Aristotelian abstraction underlies the
system of St Thomas whereas St Bonaventure, following St
Augustine, is full of Platonic notions of psychology. Quite
recently, too, we have seen Maurras and the Christian Demo-
crats basing their political philosophy upon St Thomas and
expecting the materialists to accept his definition of the consubstantial union of soul and body. No, let us not dilute the
wine of divine wisdom with water, as St Bonaventure said.[2]

Tackling the problem from the other side, from the point of
view of science and its needs, it is apparent that a form of
knowledge whose origin and rules derive from faith, that is,
independently of all evidence, cannot claim the title of a
science, however rationally and logically it is pursued, since
science is built upon clear and evident statements of fact. To

---

[2] *Pessimum miraculum*, he says, "A wretched miracle where the wine
is changed into water": *Coll. in Hex.* 19, 14–15. A lecture at Paris University, 1273, against St Thomas Aquinas.

"believe" the statements of anybody, even of God himself, is something of a quite different order. The degree of certitude we then have will depend on the character of the speaker and the amount of credence we ought to give to his words. But by the very presence of this personal factor we are outside the pale of science where objectivity, based on discovered connections between natural objects, is all-important and where personal confidence and private inclination have no place.

Faith, therefore, in communion with a self-revealing God, is rooted in authority. St Paul speaks of obedience to the faith (Rom. 1. 5). But this inner constraint has nothing in common with the constraint exercised by reason over the evidence, derived from observation or inference, which we find in science. The latter imprisons my spirit, perhaps in my own despite, whereas my submission to the authority of the primary truth is a virtue in me; my will determines my assent, and my trust and love render it delightful. Authority and reason cannot live together. What one gains the other loses. The loving docility of the believer is poles apart from the rational demands of the schoolman. Truth dwells, no doubt, on both sides, but on the one hand it is truth accepted, ready-made, on trust; on the other it is truth conquered, discovered, more and more searchingly dug out. Both will be the losers by being mingled.

Thirdly (the final objection), faith, we may say, can neither exist nor be defined without introducing the decisive factor of a personal will, a personal love; and the same must be true by inference of theology, for theology derives from an act of faith. The certainty and the content of both are based upon a testimony, the testimony of the Holy Spirit, definitively communicated by and through the authentic and authenticated utterances of the prophets and by the Church which holds the mandate of Christ. Now this testimony feeds upon personal trust and confidence, which is subjective, and where reasons have no place save within a communion which decides their validity. What one may call its "credibility" does not depend upon external guarantees (as miracles are appealed to as guarantees of the Word of God) but is a quality inherent in the One who speaks. The theologian is wholly dependent on the testimony of God, lovingly accepting the whole of it as truth. But that is a road which the scientist, as such, can never follow.

From this it follows that the act of faith is free. In fact this is its primary quality, if it be true that faith is fundamentally a communion between one person and another, without moral or intellectual constraints. Since he believes, the theologian's mind will be pervaded by this initial act of choice, quite irrespective of any motive based on (external) credibility, since no miracle or other sign from God constitutes the inward reason for his assent; that is based on the mystery itself, the Word of God.

Entry into faith, its progress, its fullness, take on the character of an *initiation*, mystically pervasive, which no mere indoctrination can satisfy. It does not reach us as a science does. We are not *taught* it, as we are taught a theorem in geometry or an electronic theory. It is a "message" which the Church of Christ brings to us. We know well that a catechism without catechesis (to use a suggestive modern play upon words) is contrary to the faith's "laws of transmission". It is not merely bad teaching but bad theology.

These objections deserve to be taken seriously. At the most intricate nexus of the problem they are drawn from the nature of faith itself and of science itself. They formulate and give meaning to that instinctive repugnance which has been noted above and which is expressed more or less forcefully both by the simple believer and even by the theologian himself. How *can* theology, an understanding of the faith, be a real science?

THEOLOGY AND FAITH

When all is said and done, these objections rest ultimately upon the following proposition: that theological science can only come to birth and grow to maturity *within* the faith. A theology without faith? Some people have attempted to imagine something of the sort, but for our part we can only regard it as a vicious infiltration of eighteenth-century rationalism into theological method. In that age of so-called enlightenment rational knowledge was exalted as the sole pattern of all knowledge, according to the principles of scientific research (in the modern sense). Along with this conception of knowledge there went also a conception of the faith, reducing it to a mere supernatural formulation of popular beliefs. Since then the philosophers have reacted against this narrow definition of human understanding and have allowed, even in their own domain, some value to belief or testimony as a way of access to certain human realities. But we, in any case, reject any similar contamination of theological knowledge by the scientific mentality. Whatever one may say about theology it certainly cannot have either meaning or content save in the light of faith.

To start with, the divine object does not exist for man except in a revelation, an unveiling, wherein God himself speaks of "that which God alone knows about himself and which he has communicated to us by revelation" (*Summa Theologica*, Ia, qu. 1, art. 6). Here is a datum which I should not have been able even to imagine without that divine *magisterium*, exercised in his Church. The acceptance of such objects of faith as his stock-in-trade, so to speak, is the theologian's first act. Are not these "articles of faith" the very rudiments of his knowledge?

Speaking more inwardly, faith is necessary in order to raise my mind to the level of an object which is by its nature inaccessible to me. Only on this level—communion with the mind of God—is a theology (*theo-logia*) not only normal but possible. In the knowledge of God, as in all knowledge, the object known is not just a kind of foreign body introduced like a stone into an organism. To know is in some sort to *become* the object. It is the realizing of a homogeneity (the scholastics, translating the inspired language of St Dionysius, called it *continuitas* or *continuatio*) which in this instance is the effect of a freely-bestowed grace. The theologian thinks and works within this homogeneity.

But might not a non-believer, if presented with the data of revelation as material for analysis, definition and deduction, practise theology? Suppose, for example, that he was given the fact of Christ's true humanity and that he drew the inference that Christ possessed human knowledge alongside of his divine knowledge, would not his reasoning be valid? Materially, yes; but in the disposition of his argument—premises, middle terms etc.—there would not flow that inner light which brings true understanding of the fact under analysis. It would be just the same with a purely critical reading of the text of Scripture, the word of God. Without faith it would be a mere nibbling at the rind (St Gregory). The work of the theologian would then not only be deprived of the requisite spiritual refinement, the spirit of faith; it would also lack a certain quality essential to it, that quality which produces in the mind what Claudel has punningly called co-birth (*co-naissance* and *connaissance*). "Treat the data of revelation as purely theoretical statements, forget the living social and psychological integument from which you disengage them, and you are likely to understand them but ill. Transform them into mere metaphysical speculations, disregard the all-pervading and infinite love of God communicating itself to men, and you will not understand them at all" (G. Rabeau). If you lose the faith you lose theology.

In truth, theology is a participation in God's own knowledge of himself: *Quaedam impressio divinae scientiae* (*Summa Theologica*, Ia, qu. 1, art. 3). Therefore if it be a science it will not become so by emptying or diminishing faith—as if the believer, by growing in understanding, might gradually drain away the mystery. Let my believing intelligence, in its quest, arm itself with all the equipment of research, let its curiosity be organized, let it develop what we may call by analogy its own scientific spirit. So be it; but this will only come to pass under the enduring efficacy of the infused light of faith.

THEOLOGY AND THEODICY

Before considering how this efficacy is conditioned and extended we may here distinguish between theology and what, since the days of Leibniz, has been called "theodicy"—although the term does not always imply adherence to Leibniz's system. The similarity of the words demands clarification.

There exists in principle, and there has existed in the past in practice, a quest for and a discovery and knowledge of God by reason alone, independently of the Christian faith. The pagan philosophers not only attempted this task; some of them, like Plato and Plotinus, raised in this field a magnificent edifice of truth and unquestionably extended the range of the contemplative life. The *Symposium* and the sixth book of the *Enneads* are masterpieces not only of dialectic but of the religious knowledge of God which will always remain valuable. In the work of these ancient masters, and also in that of many modern philosophers, not to mention the sages of India, we find not only ways of approach to the divinity and proofs of the existence of God but also a lofty philosophy whose wisdom has always been appreciated by Christians. The Church herself has declared that certain knowledge of God is possible, outside his own revelation of himself, by the light of human reason. Since the creation of the world his invisible perfections have been reflected and presented to human understanding in the things which he has made (Vatican Council, III, 2). This knowledge still remains for the most part difficult, slow, feeble and loaded with error (*ibid.*) and the history of human thought, among great and little minds alike, illustrates both this power and its limitations.

Power and limitations alike make clear the methods and characteristics of this rational knowledge of God, both in simple perception and its metaphysical development ("theodicy"). The mind proceeds from the data of cosmic and human reality, seeking its causes in order to understand the whole, thence passing beyond causes to the subject-matter of the various sciences, and so upward to the supreme cause, the cause of causes which explains the very existence of everything. Whatever the problems of this dialectic may be—epistemological, psychological or religious—its transition from the tangible to the transcendent involves, as it were, taking the brakes off the use of analogy (*analogia entis*) and it is an upward-moving quest in which man takes the initiative and applies the fruits of his study to his knowledge of the world, of himself and of his destiny. In other words God is here the object of a knowledge which for two reasons is not his own free gift—firstly because it does not proceed from his own personal initiative and secondly because it is used for the explanation of earthly things. Ultimately, a scientific investigation of nature which reaches as high as God—"the God of scientists and philosophers" (Pascal)—arises out of "Physics" in the fullest sense of that word, as St Augustine long ago remarked. If in the course of this metaphysical ascent the forces of subjective religious experience should join the dance, as happened with the neo-Platonists, there may be an admirable enrichment of the spiritual life; but the essential form and objective value of this "contemplation" still belong, even in the ecstasies of a Plotinus, to the realm of human initiative and human dialectic.

Theology, on the contrary, proceeds from God, in the most literal and personal sense. It is he who enters into a relationship with man, a relationship as between one man and another, an intimate relationship. This religion (re-ligation, renewed bond) therefore follows a road diametrically opposite to the one taken by theodicy as described above. Here God reveals himself freely, and it is only within this "grace" that man, by an act of faith, can enter into communion with him.

It follows that theodicy belongs to the order of speculation (in the wider sense of the word) based on the laws and problems of nature, whereas in theology the initiative of God realizes itself in history, his encounters with mankind stretch out over the course of time. The Judaeo-Christian revelation is no Platonic or Aristotelian treatise; it is found in sacred history, the history of the "people of God", beginning with Abraham, father of all believers, and in an historical fact, dazzling in its mystery, the birth of Christ in Bethlehem. He is the "God of Abraham, Isaac and Jacob" (Pascal). What he in liberty and love designs for us cannot be reduced to a system of logical necessity, and this is the utmost that mere speculative meditation on the divine attributes could bring forth. The difference is radical. The would-be theologian must, from start to finish, work within the faith and upon a given revelation.

Of course he will take over, with great advantage to his studies, the reasoned achievements of the metaphysician and his theodicy. Augustine feeds upon Plotinus; St Thomas studies Aristotle. There is nothing but good in this, for it presupposes that faith and reason are in some sort homogeneous, although they follow different roads towards knowledge. We shall return to this subject later on. But this does not at all diminish the radical difference, in principle and in method, between divine revelation and philosophical contemplation.

The same difference subsists, though under very different conditions, between theology and what has been called "Christian Philosophy". The expression is a controversial one because the adjective tends to swallow the noun, but what I mean is a philosophy (or philosophies) in which faith exerts itself not so much by bringing this or that conclusion into accord with Christian teaching as by more or less consciously permeating all philosophical reflection upon man and the universe with the light of divine revelation. For reason this is a delicate task. It may result, and sometimes has resulted, in hybrid products, wherein reason and faith alike corrupt one another for the sake of producing facile agreements. Yet the attempt is sound in principle, as history shows, provided that the realms of reason preserve their autonomy, albeit illumined by the light of faith.

At all events this is definitely a branch of philosophy (Cf.

infra).[3] Reason is still the formal regulator of the inquiry and the arbiter over assent and dissent, for the objects under discussion are as it were natural phenomena, not the presumed words of God. The more philosophical a Christian philosophy is, so the more theological is theology—i.e. understanding the faith in the Word of God. As with theodicy, all these fine distinctions are not just "scholastic subtlety" but sober truth concerning God and his ways. The more numerous and confident, the more necessary, the relationships between various mental disciplines become, the more important it is that they should establish and maintain their autonomy—to the benefit both of their own transcendent unity and of our own spiritual unity.

[3] The same is true of the "philosophy of religion"—a rational criticism of religion as such and of the state of mind which it engenders, irrespective of the psychological, sociological and metaphysical factors which condition it.

CHAPTER II

UNDERSTANDING THE FAITH

Quoniam rapimur amore indagandae veritatis.
For we are ravished with love for the truth
that awaits our study.
St Augustine, *de Trinitate.*

We express the faith to ourselves, didactically, in a series of
propositions which we call a "creed", and these "articles of
faith" are the authentic expression in human terms of the
Word of God. But assuredly we cannot reduce faith to a mere
recitation of verbal and conceptual truths accepted in blind
obedience. It is in these truths and through them that we are
joined in communion with the substance of the reality of God,
brought to us by his Word and through his grace—a living
participation in the knowledge God has of himself and of his
Son. Its root is the fulfilment of that love whereby God
associates us with his own life. "Faith," says St Paul, "is that
which gives substance to our hopes, which convinces us of
things we cannot see" (Heb. 11. 1) and "Faith," says Scheeben,
"presents itself as a direct intercourse, an intimate union with
the Word of God, and therefore with his inner life. And since
this inner Word did not only exist at the moment of its manifestation but exists, like the eternal Word, in an eternal present,
it lifts our minds into a participation in his truth and in his
life, and even now allows us to rest there."[1]

[1] J. Scheeben (one of the masters of the theological renaissance in
nineteenth-century Germany), *Dogmatik*, I, 40, n. 681.

This intercourse, in the mystery and the light of faith, takes on a quite unprecedented human import as soon as it is applied more precisely to that startling initiative which God took to actualize it. He did so according to a plan (an "economy" the Greek Fathers call it) completely dominated by an incarnation. To achieve this intercourse with us God does not raise us to his own level in a sublime paradise; it is he who descends to our human level. In fact the Father, to adopt us as his divine sons, sends his own and only Son so that we can find on our own level a divine life that is completely humanized. A communion has been established, one might say, as between man and man. Through the Son, God-made-man and born of a woman, we have access to the Father. It is within this system, or economy, that my faith finds its object—God himself, the ultimate truth; and it is here that theology is born within me.

It is therefore by these two means, distinct yet entirely homogeneous, that this incarnation of God is accomplished: an incarnation of the Word of God in the words of men, in the Scriptures; and an incarnation of the Son of God in a human nature, in direct contact with humanity. How wonderful this coherence is! Theologians and contemplatives of the Middle Ages used often to dwell upon it but we, since the crisis of the Reformation, have become less perceptive.

If this is so, and to the extent that it is so, in our minds or in our "hearts", as the Scriptures would say, then faith becomes in me a power whose vital intellectual force is gripped by an almost biological hunger for fulfilment—for that beatific vision of God, of which faith is the earthly bait. All the inner laws of knowledge will be brought into play in this encounter between object and subject—in this case between God-as-object and man-as-subject—which philosophers find in that great mental exercise which is called "an act of knowing".

Consider first the fertility of the object. In a revelation where the light of faith puts me on a level with his transcendence and initiates me into his mystery and incarnate mercy, the living God, the living truth, becomes for me not a mere mental object; he offers himself as a gift from the spirit in an ever more intimate communion, welcomed by love. If I am "faith-ful" and if my faith accepts this message and this trust, it nourishes me by its very presence. The mystery of faith feeds me, ·swells my understanding both of God himself and of his guidance of the universe, of mankind and of myself in the heart of mankind.

Consider next the hunger of the subject, whetted by such nourishment, at the highest pitch of intellectual curiosity. Surely the most significant and profoundest act of which our intelligence is capable is the search for causes and especially for the supreme cause. My act of faith excites in me an ardent, an insatiable desire to discover and attain that cause and to obtain from it a science, the science of God in himself and in his designs. My whole faith is possessed by this striving to-wards a vision in which I shall find, within this ever-incompre-hensible divinity, the sum of all the divine forces working for the adoption of men into God's inner life. Then indeed is faith the bait of the beatific vision, the foretaste of future bliss.

Such a process obviously cannot be an anonymous activity within some collective body where Christ would dissolve indi-vidual personalities in order to make them divine; no, it must be an inner personal relationship, as real love will relentlessly demand. The divine union of man with Christ must be between individuals, by and in a faith where the liberty of each is not only a basic condition of the union but also the delightful law of mutual love.

It is true that faith, in its earthly form, has an inherent and characteristic content—otherwise the very essence of this super-communion would dissolve—and this content is proclaimed in a series of predicates and "dogmatic formulae" which are de-fined and promulgated by the Church, the earthly mistress and teacher of this revelation. But these formulae are not the ulti-mate object of faith. Rather it is the will of faith which brings them to life and, through them, opens the soul to God. Thus faith is a light, of the same nature as the divine reality.

Herein lies the marvel of the thing: God, this object that is at once explained and inexplicable, is also the inner principle which raises my understanding to the level of the mystery. And this raising demands nothing of me, for it is achieved by love—and all love yearns for a communion. So it comes about that with certain types of knowledge the object to be known and the enlightenment which enables me to know it are one and the same. Rational investigation can, and indeed sometimes must, prepare the ground for this fundamental intimacy by an examination of its credibility, but the inner motives for its loyalty remain pure, in complete submission to the word of God addressed to me. "Faith would lose its value", says St Gregory,[2] "if human reason could supply the proofs of it."

Such, then, is the "primary" truth, according to the import that metaphysics gives to that epithet; a living truth, a *personal* truth. It has authority, a complete authority which demands spiritual obedience.

Authority in theology is not just an accidental addition; it is something fundamental to the revelation and to the truth which the believer finds in it. The facts of revelation can change my personal life, and at the same time they are the foundation of a new form of communal life. In this sense they have authority over *my* life and *our* community. The word of God is authority in its application both to my own life and to us all. Authority is something fundamental in the sphere of religion. God wants something for me and for us. This, as Cullmann has shown, is the primary meaning of the term "dogma"—a word more radical and of wider scope than "doctrine" which merely makes explicit its theoretical dimension. "Dogma" for me is of an order transcending an absolute event and, as such, includes a doctrine *in potentia*. It is by this twist that truth and authority are one. The sequence proceeds as follows: authority of the Word, authority of the Scriptures, authority of faithful teaching, authority of theology.[3]

By the same token, this authority does not assert itself by external pressure. When we adhere to this God-truth and when we then seek to understand it through theology it is not only because God has spoken it but because he knows it; and much

---

[2] *Homily on the Gospel*, 26.
[3] P. Ricœur, *Histoire et Vérité* (Paris, 1955), pp. 160–1.

only because he knows it but because it is his own knowledge of himself in which he allows me to share. Thus faith, and the theology of faith, takes the form of a personal link between mind and mind, where assent is present in me through grace and is brought about by a will for salvation. If God revealed to me mathematical, physical and historical truths there would be no part for the will to play, no place for the individual, because this link would be lacking. Modern philosophers would say that it is a question of existential knowledge. We prefer to say, in traditional language, that it is the testimony of the Spirit within us. Testimony calls for belief, an essentially personal act, which, though it be the work of intelligence and not of some vague sentimental experience, is in a different category from any impersonal "objective" acceptance of a mathematical theorem, a law of nature or even a philosophical theory. In short, the spiritual rôle of theology is the understanding of this object of faith, the *intellectus fidei*.

Thus faith, by its very nature and by the spontaneous increase of grace which it brings, is pregnant with theology. We must give this word "theology" its widest and fullest meaning: it is an understanding of God, with a penetration as simple as that of sight; it involves the fullness of a faith grown adult in the conscious attainment of its aim; it involves a knowledge as technical and well-ordered as that of a human science, and it involves a preaching of the Gospel. We do not depreciate the scientific character of theology by giving it the generic meaning, both narrow and broad, that the ancients gave to the word "theologia" with the stress rather on its mystical character than on its technical equipment, as shown particularly in the works of St Dionysius and his many followers in the east and the west.[4] The variety of these diverse aspects of

4 "Theologians", says St Dionysius, "deliver their message in two different ways: one way is mystical and inexpressible, the other is clear and accessible. The first way is symbolic and involves an initiation, the other is philosophic and works by demonstration. And so the incommunicable is grafted on to the communicable. The one is persuasive and its strength is in the strength of its words. The other, not by instruction but by initiation, establishes the soul within the Godhead" (*Letter IX*).

divine knowledge does not interrupt its objective and methodical continuity. St Thomas Aquinas is, of course, the theologian *par excellence* in the specific sense of the word, yet the Curé d'Ars also has his own theology and so too has the "little old woman" (the *Vetula* of St Thomas) who keeps the word of God and tells her beads. St Augustine is a theologian not only when he is writing his *de Trinitate* but also when giving to his people a commentary on the Gospel of St John.

Thus through the fertility of this faith all the manifold resources of the mind are quickened into life, for the divine light of faith becomes as it were incarnate in that mind. This "cogitation", as St Thomas and St Augustine have said[5]— whether by a sort of swift fermentation or by being geared into the various processes of my intellect or, better still, by both together—develops *within* the bare assent which I give to the Word of God and becomes a striving towards the understanding of what I believe. Assent does not stop at outward submission; it unleashes a curiosity in which both nature and grace are at work—the nature of intelligence and the grace of faith. It is childish to say, "I believe everything the priest tells me" unless what he teaches me is both seen in the personal light of my own faith and grappled with by my curiosity. In this way, at my own cultural level, I can take to pieces, as it were, the official teaching I have received and build it into my own thoughts and conduct.

St Thomas likens this inner multiplication of the articles of faith in theology to that of the first principles in terrestrial forms of knowledge—that is, of those principles whose content is most elementary in form and at the same time most rich and fruitful in results, such as the principles of identity, sufficient reason and final cause. That is, in theological processes at their various levels and also in their conclusions, the light of faith envelops, penetrates and redisposes the data which my mind itself has built up—either in doctrine or in morality.

If this is so, the contemplative and speculative act of the

[5] *Summa Theologica*, IIa, IIae, qu. 2, art. 1.

theologian is not only an adoration, an act of devotion, a spiritual cult, all of which are acts springing from the virtue of religion; no, the act of the theologian is more than this. It belongs to the cycle of the divine life which is formed in us by the three cardinal virtues of faith, hope and charity; and it is only within this cycle that both the speculations of the expert and the actions of the practising Christian have any truth or value. Even in its rudimentary forms theology safeguards us from the emptiness of pedagogic or sociological conformism, whether sacramental or otherwise.

Fides quaerens intellectum, faith in quest of understanding. We can now see the depths and implications of this phrase by which the great master of theology, St Anselm, defined the rôle of theology. It is not therefore an outlandish study, containing few attractions and some dangers. On the contrary, we might say that it is the healthy act of a faith whose appetite, like a physical appetite, is the measure of a healthy constitution. It is perhaps an unconscious appetite, a simple biological instinct, but if I become conscious of it and strive to control its impulses it will renew my vitality and counteract my weaknesses. Thus the appetite of faith is the begetter of theology.

Of this inner travail the Vatican Council gives the following concise description: "Reason, enlightened by faith and through attentive, zealous and sober research, acquires with the help of God's grace a very fruitful understanding of the mysteries—either through analogies with natural knowledge or through the inter-connection of the mysteries with one another or with the supreme end of man."[6] We shall have to return to this passage, but let us here and now take note that the undertaking is attributed to human reason, acting in the light of faith. In other words, the operation is conducted not by a light placed in my mind but by my mind itself—flooded, it is true, by an infused light but in accordance with its own abilities and structure.

Healthy? Balanced? Yes, even when this theological

[6] Session III, Chap. 4.

euphoria goes so far, in certain moments of grace, as to become
a sort of intoxication—an intoxication which, in view of the
inevitable imbalance brought about by communion with such
exalted realities, is legitimized precisely by the intoxicating
nature of the mystery of the divine Object. As St John Damascene has said, the theologian is swept off his feet in the vast
sea of the divine substance, for the more fully he partakes of
this Life the more he feels it to be beyond his grasp on a level
he can never reach. "Never," declared the Lateran Council,
"can there be so great a similarity between the Creator and his
creature that one cannot at the same time perceive a still
greater dissimilarity."[7] Hence these tensions. *Sobria ebrietas*:
the old expression of the Platonic philosophers comes into its
own here, in letter and in truth, human and divine. Now that
God is made man and that we are the sons of God in the
earthly brotherhood of his Son, the ecstasy of the pagan mystics
becomes wisdom.

An ancient master of theology in the twelfth century, Richard
of St Victor, in his treatise *de Trinitate* (a work which will bear
comparison with that of St Augustine) bears witness to this
intoxication and describes it on several occasions in the simplest
of terms. To those of his hearers who sniggered at their master's
exaltation and at the over-burden of dialectic with which he
loaded it he would say:

> I accept your laughter provided it is the fruit of your under-
> standing. It is true that my meditations often end in failure, but
> these setbacks only serve to spur me on, and my failures are the
> very results of my zeal. I am like Balaam's ass which delays her
> rider but is nevertheless ceaselessly spurred on her way. You
> say I cannot reach my goal? But the journey itself is a joy and
> a delight. . . . It is true that faith is the unbreakable foundation,
> but it is no more than the bait for the beatific vision; and step by
> step I press on towards this consummation of my happiness: to
> know that which I now believe, *ut intelligam quod credo*. What
> are we believers about if we do not pursue, as did even the

[7] *Inter creatorem et creaturam non potest tanta similitudo notari, quin
inter eos major sit dissimilitudo notanda.* Lateran Council, 1215.

pagan philosophers, a contemplation which exalts love in us?
It profits us little to believe the truths concerning God if we do
not exert ourselves to understand them, *comprehendere ratione
quod tenemus ex fide.* What wonder, then, if in this mystery my
soul be plunged in darkness? But in this ascension it is Christ
who leads and guides. It is he who, through his spirit which has
descended upon me, awakens me and provokes my love.[8]

Thus it is that the loftiest speculations of the theologian are
linked to the ideals of the mystic.

St Thomas, in his austerely profound language, said: "In the
ardour of his faith the Christian loves the truth which he
believes. He turns it in his mind, he embraces it, and he seeks
for all the reasons that he can find which will support this
meditation and this love."[9]

[8] Richard of St Victor, *de Trinitate*, III, 1, and Prologue, P.L., 196.
915, 889.
[9] *Summa Theologica*, IIa, IIae, qu. 2, art. 10.

CHAPTER III

THEOLOGY AND MYSTERY

The point we must needs return to is this: that theology is born, grows up and is brought to full accomplishment within the heart of the mystery—not only because its subject-matter is the mystery of God and his historical plans but also because its inner workings, even in their most intellectual forms, are wholly permeated by the mysterious light of that faith which entitles me, as has been said, to this divine communion. Theology involves an initiation—or, to use the words of Dionysius, untranslatable in the west, the theologian is a mystagogue, an initiator.

GOD'S SILENCE

In this understanding of the faith, and by the very intimacy which it implies (an intimacy to some extent humanized in Christ), we must beware of an unconscious temptation to lose sight of God's absolute transcendence and to assume a sort of rational familiarity with him in which his mystery would be degraded. God is and must remain the impenetrable; otherwise he would no longer be God.

Even when a rapport is established between God and man there is no question of any mere accidental disparity of levels in a hierarchy of objects wherein the supreme and divine object is no more than the highest among similar realities belonging to the same order. God cannot be categorized by any science or philosophy. The great masters, even among the pagans, have always laid down as an elementary law for all knowledge of God this need for a permanent superiority in him and for a constant purification of our modes of thought about him. They demonstrate the urgency of this need in their very language, not by piling on superlatives (for the superlative might appear linked to that which it surpasses) but by setting up a system of negatives (*via negativa*) which rejects the whole apparatus of positive names and titles. St Thomas expresses this with his usual moderation: "We cannot know what God is but only what he is not, and in what way everything else relates to him." And the neo-Platonists, by way of hypostatizing this negativeness so far as possible, gave the name of "Silence" to this inaccessible divinity. "No man has ever seen God," says St John (1. 18).

No question, here, of incapacity on the subject's part, of feebleness in you or me or any of us. It is the object itself which, if it exists, and even when it is shared with us, imposes this unbridgeable gulf. The very word "object" is philosophically awkward and does not fit the Absolute to the letter. He is, in fact, literally super-natural; and therefore even when this communion of love which his grace concedes me is fully realized, God will remain incomprehensible until I meet him face to face. All our efforts irrevocably revolve between two dialectical poles—proved over and over again by the Doctors of the Church. On the one hand the unmediated vision face to face (insisted on by the Latin Fathers of the lineage of St Augustine) and on the other the unrelenting incomprehensibility (stressed by the Greeks with St John Chrysostom and Dionysius). Material for academic debate? Perhaps; but more truly the authentic dual expression of the revealed mystery, of the Silence—with which, nevertheless, man may converse.

For a better understanding of this "supernatural substantiality," theology's native territory, we may make a comparison with another type of divine activity in which the supernatural element is only present in the means used—I mean in God's miraculous interventions in the natural order.

To cure a sick man suddenly, to prophesy the future, to speak an unknown language—these things surpass the laws of nature but in themselves, however awe-inspiring, they only concern earthly things—good health, the events of tomorrow, human speech—all of them things within the scope of our own intellectual and practical capabilities. A miracle involves an intervention of God that is *unusual*; but it is not in the category of "mystery".

Thus the theologian must be on his guard not only against allowing his knowledge to sink to an earthly level but also against a kind of facility, both in language and thought, which tempts him to regard his knowledge as a capital fund, earned and accumulated by himself, to be drawn upon, cashed and manipulated at his pleasure. Plato long ago denounced those babblers who, even in divinity, make a trade of words, with mocking flippancy.

In the west, the classic case of this failing is that of Abelard. This champion of dialectic was the first whose genius promulgated the laws of conceptual thinking in their application to theological knowledge. He is called, not without cause, the founder of scholastic theology. But in the intoxication of his discovery he could not maintain the proper spiritual attitude towards the awful silence of the mystery. We must recognize the validity of his method, which makes him the forerunner and guide of the great scholastic masters; but we can also understand and pardon the impatient opposition of St Bernard to this kind of irreverence—even though Abelard declared, purposefully and truthfully, that his only desire was to become a "believer", faithful to Christ rather than to philosophy. Theology can only develop in a healthy religious manner and, in the long run, without errors (cf. Abelard) if it *faithfully* welcomes the holy and sacred atmosphere of the mystery. Theology presupposes a curiosity aroused by faith, but it also demands a discretion which is not only an effect of delicacy of touch but is also the seal of the Holy Spirit. Pity the theologian (says Kierkegaard) for whom the tension of the mystery ever grows slack.

Describing the internal laws of theology, St Thomas, using some untranslatable adjectives, writes, "The principles of this science are received through revelation; thereafter, the manner of communicating these principles, which is *relativus* on the part of God who infuses them, must become *orativus* in him who receives them." It is in prayer and adoration, and in the profoundest sense of the word devotion, that theology, the understanding of the Word of God, is born and lives. "This sacred science," reads the office of Albert the Great, "is acquired through prayer and devotion rather than through study"—words not to be taken as an epigram but as a structural necessity. A theology that could be true without being devout would be a sort of monster.

BASED UPON EVIDENCE

"If one were to tell a man about things of which he had no previous knowledge, nor ever seen depicted in any way, he would know no more about them than if one had not spoken. For instance, if one assured him that on some island there was a species of animal which he had never seen and which bore no resemblance to any animal familiar to him he could conceive no idea of it, however much one told him about it. The same thing would happen if one attempted to describe the colours red and white to a man born blind." In these simple terms does St John of the Cross describe the inescapable absence of the transcendent God. What then in this mystery is the established line of communication? Of what sort is the knowledge that is founded upon faith?

It is a knowledge of evidence. I believe in the Word of God, and it is this Word which is the object of theology. The messengers and mediators of this word have changed with the various stages of the Jewish and Christian "economies"—from the prophets to the *magisterium* of the Church, passing through the Son—but theology still adheres to a word which God addresses to man, not through mediation of his creatures but as from himself, in person. The theologian, by definition, is one who hearkens to this revelation, who is alert for it.

Alert for the Word; and therefore, here again, in faith. And consequently, for this believer turned theologian, it is no mere intellectual quest but an active concentration of his whole being—not for the sake of some confusedly emotional contact but for an intellectual assimilation of the truths thus revealed. When, for example, at the heart of this revelation, the theologian acquires a knowledge of the Christ who died and rose again to life, he is not dealing with an historical fact of the past which a strict inquiry into the documentary evidence has established. On the contrary (though without detriment to the historical truth) he is dealing with another kind of truth, a truth of "salvation" through which my very being is linked to that death and to that resurrection. It is primarily this *appropriation* which faith brings about within me. My existence takes on a new meaning, given to it by the revelation, with the result that my conviction does not spring from any rational discovery but from the very science of God. The rationalist Lessing rightly refused to pass from the historic proof of the objective event of Christ's resurrection to the personal and "engaging" truth of faith.[1] Indeed, it is the besetting vice of a certain type of intellectual (Benda, Maurras, Valéry) to recognize even on the human plane only one type of valid knowledge, and to reject with scorn any belief or knowledge based on evidence—even God's own evidence about himself. In their eyes all this is infected by freedom of assent, and by

---

[1] Lessing, *Ueber den Beweis des Geistes*, ed. Petersen, Vol. 20, p. 48. "I willingly believe that Christ, against whose resurrection I have no historical objections to offer, represented himself to be the Son of God, and was so accepted by his disciples. These are truths which, belonging as they do to one and the same class, follow naturally one from another. But to leap from this historical truth over to an altogether different class of truths, and to expect me to revolutionize all my moral and metaphysical ideas merely because I can offer no credit-worthy evidence against the fact of Christ's resurrection—if this is not a μετάβασις ἐις ἄλλο γενος (an improper transposition from one category to another) then I know not what Aristotle meant by that expression."

love; and thereby the very possibility of a theology is abolished.

Yet if evidence be given by one person to another (including that given through an authentic and necessary mediator) it is very important to note that the theologian, when elaborating the content of the Word of God, goes beyond the borders of a simple act of faith. In the following chapter we shall have to insist on the differences between faith and theology. For the present we merely remark that theological reasoning, by the very fact that it elaborates, analyses and reconstructs the data of faith, transforms faith's content from a simple and personal *hearing* of the Word into a universal expression of it. This expression is, of course, still answerable to the tribunal, to the criteria, of faith, but it does constitute what is called a theological datum. It is not merely valid for me privately but is *communicable* by teaching. And therefore, we maintain, theology is a science.

It remains true that, to ensure continuity between faith and theology, the Word of God must remain present to me both objectively as an accepted truth and subjectively in my personal knowledge. Furthermore I do not find this Word only in archaic and sacred texts which date from an increasingly distant past. I find it today, in the daily reading of the Gospels. I find it in the Church—for the Church, the community of believers, is a real and visible society linked to Christ by the apostolic succession, the store-house and dispensary of the revelation, and the dwelling-place of the Spirit according to Christ's promise. It is here that the Word is present to me, here for my faith to hearken to it and for my mind to build from it a theological system. The Church is the spiritual home of the theologian, who finds in her both his material and his light. That too we shall have to define, and speedily, so as to proclaim the presence of the Gospel, of the Word of God, and of the spirit.

GOSPEL AND THEOLOGY

It follows from what has been said that the Scriptures are not for the theologian a mere preliminary to his real work, preceding it and outside of it, the raw material which he will have to bring to a kind of abstract maturity. The study of Scripture is not, as has sometimes been said, a science auxiliary to theology; rather is it its very soul, alive and always fresh. Indeed, history shows us in the most striking manner that a return to the Gospel has always been rejuvenating and cleansing for theology and the awakenings it has caused were not the result of external pressure but were inner awakenings of theological contemplation itself, as also in the teaching of the faith. It is no mere coincidence that the great age of theological science in the western world of the Middle Ages was also the age of evangelism by the mendicant friars, and that the great masters of this knowledge were the disciples of St Francis and St Dominic.

How true this is may be seen in the demand which has been apparent lately for a theology that is in some sort linked to evangelism, to the preaching of the faith, to the primary *facts* of salvation, to the proclamation of the Good News to the world, to the *kerygma*, to borrow a term from the Greek Bible. Theology must, of course, be didactic and suited to use in schools, but it must also, if a proper balance is to be preserved, spring from the Gospels; it must proceed as far as it can in a rational form from the apostolic teaching and then, in due course, return to it. It is regrettable but true that a certain well-known encyclopedia contains no article at all on Christ's Ascension (though devoting twelve columns to the Assumption of Our Lady) and under the heading of Easter it deals only with the ancient controversies concerning its date. There is also a treatise on dogma which contains not one paragraph about the resurrection of Christ and only mentions the *parousia* in order to denounce the eschatological views of Loisy. A painful manifestation, this, of how the theology of 1900 could lose sight of the fundamental facts of the Christian mystery.

St Thomas illustrates this need for a continual return to the Gospel message by an analogy borrowed once again from the spiritual life. Our intelligence cannot and must not be content with a rational analysis wherein reality is subjected to a process of successive abstraction. However necessary and valid this may be so far as it goes it does tend towards a dangerous idealism. We must, by a fresh synthesis, return to a direct perception, both unified and unifying, of the truth of things in their unity—a unity apart from which they would not exist. Therefore, says the Angelic Doctor, it is supremely important that theology, of all mental disciplines, should proceed to this "re-solution" and not succumb to a dull complacency with its former "compositions".[2]

We have good reasons for underlining the pastoral as well as the scientific implications of this position both in the sphere of theology and of catechesis. Fundamentally both are "biblical". "The rôle of the Word of God is not to prove theological theories; it is for theological reflection to penetrate and give intelligible expression to the Word—already accepted in faith for its own sake."[3]

It is not, however, by any means legitimate to deduce from this continual and dynamic presence of the Gospel in all doctrinal development that there should therefore be an independent "kerygmatic" theology distinct from a so-called "scholastic" theology. Such a schism would be disastrous— although it might appeal to anti-intellectualists or to fanatically "practical" evangelists who fail to appreciate the full profundity of truth which the revealed message contains.

A comparable blunder is made by those who wish to separate the work of cataloguing and analysing the content of the Word of God ("positive" theology, to use a term current in the sixteenth century and later) from the elaboration of it by our own mental resources ("speculative" theology). These functions are not only complementary but are inwardly and permanently linked together from the moment the Word of God reaches us in human words. The mere reading of it, and its translation into my own language, are facts already preg-

[2] *Comm. in Boetium de Trinitate*, q. 6, art. 1.
[3] P. Hitz, "Théologie et catéchèse" in the *Nouvelle revue théologique*, 87 (1955), pp. 908–9.

nant with conceptual elaboration. Are not whole systems built upon the interpretation of one text?

So let us show the same zeal as that which now animates pastoral theology (yes, it *is* "theology") in seeking out the laws which govern not only the practical efficacy but also the truthful transmission of the Word. From a "catechism" which was often no more than a popular version of academic theology, with its technical and impersonal language, let us turn towards a "catechesis" that is actively continuous with the Word of God, present in the mystery of the Church, and as it were fulfilled in the sacraments.

Catechesis, in its proper function, is not theology. But let us at least understand how true—religiously and intellectually— is the tradition which says that the liturgy, both in its text and still more in its exercise, is a rich pasture for the theologian. Here is no mere picturesque illustration. Here is something which follows naturally from that knowledge whose object is the divine mystery realized in the Blessed Sacrament. There can be no doubt at all that Pius XII's liturgical revival of the Easter Vigil has fostered a more lucid theology of the resurrection; for theology is the science of salvation. One enters it by an "initiation", and for this the liturgy provides both the ritual and the light. Once again we see that theology remains *within* the mystery.

There is however a gap to be bridged between the Gospel and theology. The continuity which we have claimed is not achieved without some mental and religious effort. The form in which the texts themselves is presented to us affords sufficient evidence of this—not only with regard to their literary form but also in the texture of the words themselves. The biblical vocabulary is not quite on all fours with the concepts later elaborated by the theologian, not merely because of the images and metaphors used in the sacred language but also because its basic categories express an order of things which do not spring from nature or from reason—categories, for instance, as are expressed in such terms as covenant, kingdom, judgement, glory, *parousia*, flesh, spirit, world, mission and so forth. At the beginning of the great scholastic period Gregory IX, in the foundation-charter of the young university of Paris (1231), energetically put the teachers of theology on their guard against the seductiveness of ideas whose origin and texture was philosophical. He severely reprimands those who from "theologians" grow to be "theophants". And it is precisely the fact that the Christian mystery is rooted in the religious language of the Bible which makes it possible, and will always make it possible, to translate that mystery into the language of theology—ancient and modern. St Thomas's *Summa* was in fact founded simply upon a commentary on the Gospels which was included in the ordinary course of study for Dominican teachers in the universities of Paris and Naples.

In a very suggestive allegory, St Thomas gives a symbolic description of the theologian confronted with the mystery of God. Calling to mind Jacob's struggle with the angel he writes:

> The whole night they wrestled, muscles straining, neither yielding; but at daybreak the angel disappeared, apparently leaving the field clear to his adversary. But Jacob then felt a violent pain in his thigh. He was left wounded and limping. It is thus that the theologian grapples with the mystery when God brings him face to face with it. He is taut, like a bent bow, grappling with human language; he struggles like a wrestler; he even seems to win the mastery. But then he feels a weakness, a weakness at once painful and delicious, for to be thus defeated is in fact the proof that his combat was divine.

CHAPTER IV

THEOLOGICAL SCIENCE

Having thus irrevocably established the methodological, psychological, religious and mystical continuity between theology and faith—in the presence of God's Word, in the Church's teaching of the revelation and in the promised power of the Holy Spirit—it now behoves us to determine more precisely the part played by the theologian within the manifold operations of faith, and to define the nature of that rôle in respect of its structure, its function and its value.

Can the theologian, in his understanding of the faith (cf. Chap. II) go so far as to build up a knowledge which, when fully expounded, might deserve the name of "science"? Among the answers of the experts we find both agreement and disagreement. They are alike in that all agree, from the very nature of their work and thought, that the rôle of theology must normally involve the valid and fruitful task of rationally and systematically using the methods and resources of the intellect in accordance with the capacity thereof; they disagree, however, about the precise designation and qualification of this work in its full "scientific" significance. St Thomas, when the question was posed by the rise of scholastic theology, considered that when all factors had been duly weighed and pondered it was justifiable to classify theology as a science—or, more accurately, that "sacred doctrine" in its traditional meaning included the functions of a science in its broadest epistemological sense. That too is my own opinion, and this is not just a matter for subtle controversy amongst experts. It is a point of view which, within the liberty of opinion which the Church allows, can have far-reaching repercussions—not only in the schools but also in the spiritual life, in apostolic action and in the actual presence of Christianity in the world. Even those who reject St Thomas's view (following St Bonaventure and others) will still be able to profit from a rigorous analysis of the forces and structure of what I have called an understanding of the faith, and which I shall now change slightly by calling it "theological reasoning".

THEOLOGICAL REASONING

First, for the revelation itself—not merely as a fundamental announcement, but as a *presence*, in the faith and in the Church, with all the undiluted realism and silent persistence which this word implies for a believer. It is on this "presence" that we can now build.

The theologian is a man who dares to put into human words the Word of God. Once he has heard this Word he possesses it, or rather it possesses him, and to such an extent that he thinks through it and in it, that it becomes his own thought. God's gift is a total gift. It becomes human property. Faith is a *habitus* (to use the untranslatable Latin). It is not an extraordinary *charisma*, excluded by its transcendent character from the scope of human thought. It is rather the incarnation of divine truth in the very fabric of our minds. It is not a simple trust, like Luther's *fiducia*, but a "virtue" that is embedded in us in the same way that a force is lodged in nature. Faith has its dwelling *within* reason, and it is thus entitled to "theologize" ($\theta\epsilon o\lambda o\gamma\hat{\epsilon}\iota\nu$, to speak about God). It is not that "our old man" (Rom. 6. 6) springs out of his impotence before the mystery of God. The theologian is the "new man", and in the rational and scientific elaboration of the content of his faith he still remains this "new man", in fact he brings that rôle to consummation. It is by engendering theology that faith finds the true logic of its perfection.

The progress of logic thereafter is inevitable. With all due foresight and discretion the techniques of reasoning will be set in motion: conceptual analyses, definitions and sub-divisions, classifications, inferences, rational search for explanations—all adding up to a "deduction", inasmuch as deduction is the characteristic operation of science wherein the process of rationalization achieves its fullest effectiveness. There will, of course, be symptoms of weakness in the result, but at the same time there have also been significant examples of fearless reasoning, and the "theological conclusion" em-braces both. Gains and risks go hand in hand, as we shall see. This is the dialectic of faith, its power made perfect in infirmity. The same law which once made us ask for the incarnation of God's Word in human words and on the stage of history now makes us accept in full the whole corpus of knowledge which this incarnation must imply. Theology is at one with the theandric mystery of the Word of God, the Word made flesh. There alone can it dare to find confidence in the coherence of faith and reason.

Theological science cannot therefore be formed from a col-lection of opinions that ignore the revelation, opinions to be chosen at one's own sweet will provided only that orthodoxy be satisfied. This would be a pitiful alliance of legalistic faith with vacuity of mind. No, pure reason, theological reason, must bring with it all its resources, including its power to reach conclusions. This is why philosophy, which is organized reasoning, has played such a large part in the history of Chris-tian thought and spirituality. Those who are alarmed by scholastic rationalism have only to consider the life and thought of such men as Clement of Alexandria, Origen, Dionysius, Augustine, Anselm, Bonaventure, Thomas Aquinas or Duns Scotus. To be sure there are some people who would like to purge away the philosophies of these masters, calling them Platonist or Aristotelian blemishes on the purity of their Christian spirituality. But this is the same old error—of regard-ing theology as something outside the faith, banished by its intellectualism from the very realm of faith; whereas it is in truth produced within the human mind by the very incarnation of that faith.

There is, moreover, a "science" of Christian perfection. *Moral* theology is properly and precisely that. It is not a mere collection of problems of conscience to be posed by reference to certain precepts and solved according to the degrees of acceptability of various cited authorities. That would be mere unreasoning and soulless legalism, rejected by all truly spiritual men and, in short, by all good Christians.

Humbly, therefore, and religiously, do we devote ourselves to the deduction of the divine attributes, to the construction of a treatise on the Trinity based on the idea of the procession of Persons, to a knowledge of the sacramental system which symbolically incorporates the typical actions of human life, to a moral analysis of the supernatural life of grace rendered comprehensible by the theological virtues and by the gifts of the Holy Spirit according to the psychological make-up of human beings. It is here that we see the marvel of the divine light taking possession of the mind. This is no mere dialectical scaffolding but an inner framework created by faith itself in its all-divine, all-human intellectual health. Faith, in its communion with the science of God, dares to seek reasons for God's works and thus to obtain some understanding of his mystery. *Fides quaerens intellectum.*

If reason, then, be so intimate and inward a part of theology it would seem to be a strange restriction of its power to apply it only to the defence of doctrine and to use its rational strength only to fortify the outworks of the citadel. The nineteenth century gave an inflated importance to apologetics, often at the price of weakening theology itself.[1] In contrast to this attitude we prefer to think of reason as pregnant with sacred doctrine,

---

[1] The encounter between faith and the philosophies and sciences of humanism sets problems for the theologian which run parallel to those of the ordinary Christian living in the world. But the *need* for apologetics must not lead us into making apologetics a substitute for "understanding the faith".

as the womb of sacred doctrine. No need for dogmatizing, in season and out of season, in order to appreciate the Christian structure and quality of such theological concepts as sacrament, instrumental cause, Person, generation, outward form, gift of the Spirit and so forth.

THE WORK OF THEOLOGICAL REASONING

"The kingdom of heaven is like . . ." What is the exact meaning of this kingdom of heaven, represented in so many different ways in the parables?

"The blood of the Covenant." Into what category—doctrinal, historical, legal or mystical—can we place this covenant which can simultaneously embrace all God's plans?

"We have found the Messiah." Is this the king, the son of David? The servant of Yahweh? The angel of the Apocalypse? God our saviour? How can we represent this divine person in a way that shall be all-embracing?

"The Son of Man has nowhere to rest his head." Must this be taken literally?

"Mary, mother of Jesus, is the mother of God." How can one word cover this unique and twofold reality?

"I am who am." Thus does God define himself, introducing us to his mystery by a verbal riddle.

"We say that the Creator-God is *artifex mundi*." Is this Latin word the right one to give us an understanding of the unique act of creation?

"Trinity." St Augustine has suggested that this word is too abstract to proclaim the life of the Father in the Son and the Holy Ghost.

"Jesus descended into hell." What is the truth behind this image?

"Blessed are the poor." But who, economically, mystically or ascetically, are the "poor" of the kingdom of God?

"Humility." It is a word which the moralist finds hard to classify. Do we not need faith to understand it?

One could find endless examples like these. From our first reading of the Bible and its derivatives, and in our study of their texts, we find ourselves already engaged in the first task of theological reasoning. It may appear a rough and ready business, but from commonplace meanings we are led on to symbolism and thence into mystery, and thus begins a quest which we can never abandon. We are already theologians, without knowing it. There are so many parallels and etymological niceties, so much assimilation and complication of images, and so many intellectual scalpels with which to dissect the body of the text that my curiosity must needs embrace such things as scriptural contexts and grammatical analyses. If we pursue this task and organize its results we find ourselves with a sort of theological lexicon which Christians throughout the centuries have been ceaselessly renewing.

Beneath these gradually elaborated concepts, however, it is the language itself which chiefly concerns us. The slightest transfer from one language to another is enough to make us aware of this, and even now translations of the Semitic original can hardly hope to preserve all its religious depth. Rufinus' translation of Origen, for example, is not without mistakes. It was over the too-literal translation of one word that friction occurred between Alexandria and Rome (the controversy between Pope Dionysius and his namesake the bishop of Alexandria, who was reacting against the apparently Sabellian vocabulary of Rome). The western teachers in the Middle Ages attempted three or four times to transplant the ideas of Dionysius the Areopagite, but never quite succeeded in gaining full acceptance for them. The ill-omened division between east and west arose from a confusion of terminology, the outward sign of incompatibility of mind. The expansion of the faith outside the established realms of Christendom has always presented delicate problems of communication—how to deliver the Gospel accurately yet at the same time intelligibly to new peoples. Even today, framed as it is in a Graeco-Latin vocabulary, the evangelic truth remains almost a sealed book to other civilizations—although when originally expressed it had favoured formulation in Semitic terms. Even within the western world the people's access to liturgical texts, those worthy conveyors of the living faith, presents a difficult task which, beneath its philological guise, is really a theological problem. "Scholastic" theology itself appears to be primarily a language, a learned and technical language, as contrasted with patristic and monastic theology which, nevertheless, it would be improper to stigmatize as imprecise.

All this is not a mere anxiety for exactitude and orthodoxy. It is a concern for the life and soul of words and metaphors, an anxiety for the very light of faith itself. If the Christian plan or "economy" is accomplished through the Word of God in a revelation adapted to human speech and human truth then it is both natural and necessary that the actual words should take priority in the conditions of worldly intercourse. God remains a stranger to the people whose language the missionary speaks no better than a passing traveller, and his truth finds no place in a school where grammar and exegesis are neglected. From this simple origin arises the Church's attachment to dogmatic formulas. Words, in which the faith takes flesh, are the raw material not only of the catechist but also of the professional theologian. One might even say that the theologian is primarily a philologist from the moment he seeks to understand and to elaborate his belief. Yet he creates for himself, while using the common phonetic apparatus, an original language; for the divine light will impregnate the fabric of his words—not through a relapse into sentimental pietism, as sometimes happens, but by reason of an urgent need for understanding in a faith whose very expression in verbal form involves a sort of exile, the exile of a Christian in a non-Christian world. The language of theology should be "sacred". Nothing would be more deceptive nor more intellectually perverse than to study these theological texts without remaining in secret communication with the Word of God and being as it were immersed in contemplation. Not that we advocate an "esoteric" attitude.

That is something repugnant to any true believer. By "secret communication" we mean that supreme sensitivity in faith which may declare itself not only in the language of the mystics but also in the vocabulary of the prophets, of the analytic theologian or of the humblest believer when he testifies to the truth. How unerring is the tact of the Holy Spirit, allotting even to the most rudimentary use of reason its appropriate linguistic tools, and commanding the respect and awe of the most learned scholar.

From the definition of terms, as the logicians say, we pass to the definition of things. That is to say that in the objects of faith, just as in natural objects, we are forever (even if unconsciously) in search of the causes, inner natures and origins which underlie perceptible appearances. One does not have to be a philosopher in order to pursue these definitions, in which causes find organic expression. Theology, therefore, in accordance with the dictates of intelligence, will follow the laws which govern all forms of human knowledge. It will always strive to define its objects—even God himself whom it knows to be indefinable. Such definitions, in a general sense, will indicate the scope, properties and structure of the objects in question and will also, if possible, give a technical description of their component elements.

Jesus is the Son of God—a God whose true name is Father. What is the significance of these words, borrowed from the human conception of "generation"? Can we dare to describe the indescribably intimate life of God? St Thomas sets himself this very task (e.g. in the *Summa Contra Gentiles*, IV, 10–11). The Scriptures do not present us with this concept of generation in abstract form, and the many realistic images of the birth of the children of men should warn us, as well as the Jews, against applying this idea to the life of God. Nevertheless, these words Father and Son cannot be treated as mere metaphors, bound up as they are with the physical reality of the Incarnation. St Thomas accordingly undertakes a tripartite discussion which leads him to "define" how God—pure spirit and perfection of unqualified Being—might, by generating a "Word" within himself, produce that which should possess *humano modo* the properties of a Person "begotten of God".

The Father, the Son and the Holy Ghost are "persons". This is another non-scriptural term, and its human significance, both in its breadth and its limitations, made St Augustine careful when he used it. We speak of a *person* in God for want of a better word and to avoid remaining silent. But how is this? Is there any believer who does not regard Jesus Christ as a "person"? Maybe not; but the theologian, so soon as he starts to think about the matter, finds himself in the toils of conceptual definition: What is a "person"? What does the fact of being a person add to a nature? How does existential independence enter into this concept? This is the cue for metaphysical analyses, and contradictory ones, to enter upon the scene. Boethius, operating on the borderland of philosophy and faith, had proposed a very fair definition: *Persona est rationalis naturae individua substantia*—"a person is an individual substance of a rational nature". But each of these terms is unintelligible unless it is defined in its turn, and each definition presupposes a theory which can only be expounded through another series of definitions. The theologians then observed the inadequacy of the Boethian definition when applied to God. This is a philosopher's definition, they said, formulated without benefit of the light of faith. So they sought to substitute another —either on entirely fresh lines or else by profoundly modifying the Boethian one. And so from century to century the theological work goes on, down to the minutest subtleties; yet all this is brought about by the ordinary needs of the rational appetite of faith. Any indiscretions are but accidental, though troublesome, irregularities.

Suppose, for instance, that I am tackling the problem of free will and grace and trying to define how the human will remains free even under the compelling power of the grace of God. My analysis will perforce involve a whole philosophy of man

as soon as I seek for a reconciliation between providence and
free will in the submission of lover to beloved. Here is a twofold mystery and a twofold liberty. Theologians, we know,
have disagreed about this, even to the point of violent argument. Nor is this a purely academic problem. The Molinism of
St Francis de Sales leads to a quite different sort of "spirituality" from that of St Francis of Assisi (with his interest in
evangelism) or of St Thomas Aquinas (who stressed the "free
gift" character of grace). By different definitions of liberty,
theologians have brought to birth different conceptions of
Christian humanism.

The ordinary believer, of course, adheres to the Word of
God and professes his faith without ever coming across these
scientific definitions—just as a child will use such ideas as
number, equality and function without ever having studied
higher mathematics, or as a mother will love her child without
having studied the psychology of affective complexes.

It is also true, and important to remember, that such definitions cannot be applied to God *de plano*. Does not our respect
for the mystery weaken our efforts at reasoning to the extent
of imposing upon us a mute adoration and an admission that
all we can say must be equivocal? It is here that we find,
throughout the history of Christian thought, a tension between
those whom we call mystics, that is, theologians with a greater
awareness of the ineffability of the mystery, and those whom
we call scholastics, that is, theologians devoted to expressing
the tenets of their faith in a rational and structural form. On
the one hand this tension can lead to a dangerous agnosticism[2]
and a lapse into nominalism of which Thomas à Kempis and
Gerson, for example, were suspected, and, on the other hand,
to a "theologism" in which the mystery of the Word of God
is obliterated behind dialectical scaffolding. Yet the tension
is a beneficent one when rightly poised. The fruit of it, mystical

[2] Agnosticism, that is, in the technical, not the popular sense, i.e.
agnosis, lack of knowledge.

and scholastic, may be found in full maturity in that wonderful work of the Pseudo-Areopagite, the *Treatise of the Divine Names*. From Augustine to Dionysius, and through the critical teaching of such men as Gilbert de la Porrée and Peter Lombard there developed in western theology a method of "transference" whereby the vocabulary and the concepts of man may be used to express the reality of God, both in his inward mystery and in his historical plan for our salvation. The vocabulary derives from the Bible, the concepts from human reason, and both alike were applied *analogically* so as to bridge, in some sort, the gulf between the human and divine and thereby find a way—the *via negativa*, the *via eminentiae* beloved of the mystics—whereby the human mind might know and truthfully declare the mysteries revealed in the Word of God. *Tamquam ignotus cognoscitur* (St Thomas, following Dionysius).

The laws governing this process of "analogy", and the measure of its efficacy, have doubtless been the subject of lengthy debate in the schools, and the professionals are by no means in full accord with one another, either in their mentality or in their conclusions. This is the price extorted by the mystery, for no method of reasoning, however subtle, can ever penetrate it. But these divagations—which have continued down to our own day—between the two quicksands of agnosticism and theologism in no way mar the technical skill and exquisite spiritual perceptiveness of that masterpiece of theology, the *Treatise of the Divine Names*.

The work of theological reasoning proceeds from a foundation of definitions to a superstructure of analysis, classification, division, distinction and all those other operations which tend to bring order, if only a descriptive order, into the content of the Word of God and of that Christian way of life which gives it reality in human society.

Among the many subdivisions of this task let us take as an example the subject of moral virtues. These qualities which perfect the human soul at all levels—in its functions, faculties and actions—may be penetrated by the divine light of grace. They are therefore fit subject-matter for the theologian. He can take cognizance of, and pass judgement upon, not only those virtues called "theological" which raise the innermost depths of the soul to the level of the godhead, but also those virtues which are called "infused" moral virtues and which, by a sort of inner transmutation, make human powers capable of seeking goals that are divine. The theologian, taking the revealed Scriptures, the teaching of the Church and the examples of the saints as his point of departure, can detect even in the most trivial actions the operation of these virtues. He discovers their laws and determines their criteria. He observes, classifies, compares, articulates; and he will not disdain to use—always under the clear, controlling light of faith—the conclusions of secular psychology.

Once again we shall find divergences, in methods, aims and results, between different fellow-theologians. St Thomas, filled with his conviction that grace does not repress nature but perfects it, brings the thoughts and conclusions of philosophy massively to bear upon the theology of virtue and the Christian life. His masterpiece in this line is the treatise on prudence—the most balanced and most boldly human of his writings on supernatural morality. Aristotle, corrected and reorientated, furnishes it with the basis of a "practical reason" which is to regulate all our actions and bring the light of absolute Christian values even into the shifting realm of human liberty. On the other side, however, we find that the *Imitation of Christ* in a famous chapter (III, 54) prefers to contrast, dramatically, the promptings of nature and the promptings of grace in all that concerns the spiritual life. It piously evades involvement in all these analyses and definitions. "What does it profit me to know the nature of repentance if I do not repent?" There is in this a seductive supernaturalism, but such an empirical approach is perhaps somewhat facile.

For (in this sphere even more than in others) however

vehemently one may reject the aid of human philosophy, that
very rejection is itself a philosophical act. Consciously or not,
the conception a man has of nature and humanity will enter
into the fabric of his theology. For a man who rejects any form
of dualism and maintains the substantial union of body and
soul the passions will be normal and necessary elements in
human morality. For a man who gives preeminence to the will,
a morality of duty and obedience to authority will nourish
a spirituality wherein self-mastery no longer controls a
spontaneous and inward striving towards the final goal. A
philosophy which regards social life as an essential part of
human nature and its perfection will foster a theology in which
the personal character of grace will never be allowed to
degenerate into individualistic pietism. Thus does faith supply
not only a method by which the data of revelation may be
worked out and conceptualized; it also supplies, even in the
domain of theology itself, material for an ideology, for a
rational view of the world, mankind and history, which determines both the conclusions themselves and the spirit in which
they are arrived at.

Another example, and another rôle of theological reasoning,
is to be found in the doubly sacred realm of the sacraments—
those symbolic actions which bring to pass what they signify,
bring into the religion and life of each of us the acts of Christ
himself and build up his mystical body, the Church. Here we
have a very complex ensemble—complex in itself because it
varies according to the organic needs of grace in the life of a
man as it unfolds itself, complex in the rituals which provide
its biblical and liturgical context, and complex in its history, in
the course of which its rites have been developed or renewed
for the better expression of the mysteries. We should be wrong
to limit the theologian's task to a mere definition and enumeration of the seven sacraments, leaving the practice of them to be
controlled by those who administer them, the liturgiologists
or the casuists. Theologians have always made it their business
to explore the whole territory of this universe of symbols—to

interpret its images, classify its values and discern the ritual and moral conditions of its structure in individuals or in a community. The liturgical revival in our own time derives its power from sources far beyond mere pastoral convenience or delight in splendour. It is the fine fruit of an understanding of the mystery of Christ, an understanding both rational and mystical, empirical and doctrinal. Nothing less will suffice to preserve the true balance of religion and the profound *mystique* of ritual from their two great enemies—superstition and soulless routine. In return, the theologian regards the liturgy as the special sanctuary of the faith, where the Church proclaims her message even while she prays.

In considering the theologian's tools, his equipment for reasoning, there is no real justification for dealing separately with the technique of "drawing distinctions", for this is one of the habitual tools of anyone who makes any sort of analysis in any sphere of study. Nevertheless, for all that this *distinguo* is a normal and necessary pre-requisite for precision in any branch of reasoning, it is justifiably considered especially characteristic of scholastic reasoning, and it is a fact that the art of drawing distinctions is constantly practised by all the masters of the Schools. Many of the articles in St Thomas's *Summa* are explicitly based on a structure of *Uno modo ... Alio modo*, and the answers almost always amount to a distinction by which we can measure the import and scope of a solution suggested in the body of the article. Thus, in the very process of reasoning, terms and propositions are precisely defined.

This art was, to be sure, sometimes carried to excess. The later and lesser scholastics tended to replace sound and sane analysis by sheer formalism, and it was as a result of this vice that the word "subtlety" acquired a pejorative sense which is absent from the Latin *subtilis*. Applied to Scotus by his disciples, the epithet served to flatter him, for it did not in fact refer merely to his mental agility but to the system based on his famous "formal distinction" according to which, within the unity of a concrete subject, there exist "formalities" which are truly distinct and objectively real. Herein lies the capital importance, in metaphysics and therefore in theology, of a particular type of analysis and abstraction which Thomists reject.

Abelard had been the father of scholasticism especially in this, that he had as it were imprisoned the theologian in a rationalistic cage, compelling him to distinguish the meanings of words and the ambiguity of propositions in the traditional texts set out in the form of *Sic et non*. This is a dangerous sort of dialectic, as he found. It introduces a spirit of criticism into the mystery of faith. Nevertheless, its outcome was a whole art of theological thinking—at any rate as soon as this dialectic was supported, after a study of Aristotle, by a genuine science of the mind. Theology was then already becoming a "science".

At this point the *distinguo* becomes no longer a method, simply, of resolving inconsistencies in scriptural, patristic or other texts. It unfolds a philosophy, or rather a fixed philosophical mentality. One can obtain a better idea of this by comparing the scholastic method of St Thomas, for example, with the ways of St Augustine. For the latter, things are not primarily distinct from one another but are linked together in an interlocking complex of relationships and analogies—symbolisms, in fact; they echo one another, like notes of music. Unity predominates rather than distinction, for distinction, if carried too far, would dismember and disarticulate reality. It is a philosophy of participation, concerned with the relationships between beings rather than with their separate existence, with exemplars rather than with causes. Scholastic logic, on the other hand, is one which determines and identifies; and definition, equipped with distinctions which either prepare the ground for it or constitute it, is its main task. To appreciate this difference it is sufficient to observe the way in which St Thomas interprets texts of the Augustinian type. He clarifies and distils their scientific qualities but he dims that aura of spiritual and literary significance which enriches their superficial meaning. It is not a question of precisely formulating thoughts which, without such formulation, would have remained primitive despite their Augustinian eloquence. Some of the scholastics, with a touch of disdain towards St Augustine, do seem to say as much. But it is really a question of radically different mental attitudes which have their own special ways of analysing reality.

Thus reality will take on very different colours when viewed by different minds. The nature of their objects will decide the independence of different spheres of study, within a "wisdom" which, if it claimed totalitarian authority, would lead it into a self-destructive intellectual absolutism and a political theocracy. Augustinianism has always tended in this direction, and what is today called "integrism" is a supernaturalist apparatus of authoritarianism which both the spirit and the teaching of St Thomas would reject. The art of "distinction" is certainly not gratuitous hair-splitting; it is a symptom and an effect of health in theological reasoning.

THEOLOGY AND REASON

It has been necessary to insist on the extent and diversity of these activities of reason in search of its "understanding of the faith" because some text-books, by their mode of presentation, have provoked an over-simplification which relegates the theologian to the task of merely formulating a set of syllogisms and "conclusions" which lead into a realm reserved for learned professors, outside of and beyond the domain of Holy Scripture. This displacement of values, as a result of which many people came to separate, to some extent, the knowledge of revelation in the light of faith from the "proper" object of theology, conceived as a set of conclusions obtained by deduction, has recently provoked a strong reaction. No; the aim of the theologian remains from start to finish the attainment of a beatifying knowledge of God and a full life of grace in the world.

Reasoning, then, is a major operation in theology if, in this as in other forms of knowledge, it provides the means of reaching an understanding of things and their causes. *Cursus causae in causatum.* St Thomas is here borrowing a metaphor from a Jewish thinker, a metaphor which expresses the movement or *cursus* of a mind which, being incarnate in a body and therefore bound to time and space, is necessarily a reasoning mind and thus constrained to *discursus*. "Why?" is the constant question of our irrepressible instinctive curiosity, even in what concerns God himself.

Why did God create the world? And why, in this world, did he create man? From the moment he asks this elementary question the Christian, the reasoning Christian, is possessed by a need for enlightenment and by the certainty of a mystery. Will he imagine a God who has to cogitate over his plans as a man would, weighing up various factors like a craftsman? First steps are feeble. This conception will have to shed its anthropomorphism—whether it imagines God as acting with the capricious vagueness of a man or whether it fetters his divinity with some theory of "inner constraint" or "necessary emanation". Faith teaches me that the act of creation was a free act. This is no mere rule of orthodoxy but a result of retrospective thought which enables me to appreciate the absolute freedom of a creative love. From this I can go on to deduce the idea of a unique relationship between creator and creature in which "necessity" can play no part save on the creature's side.

Why did God become man? From the naïve question of the catechumen down to the great controversies between Thomists and Scotists on the motive behind the Incarnation, faith's pressure on us is relentless. The growing subtlety of the quest serves only to bring to light the inspired profundity of both parties to the debate. They do not contradict each other, but one side is more concerned with the fact of man's disaster which attracted God's loving help, whereas the other sees in the first-born of every creature the attainment of a universe thus made divine.

When it sets out in search of principles for the solution of its problems the discursive intelligence deploys its forces on a fairly wide front, even though it may not always establish in this field any "demonstrations" properly so called. But such preliminary deployments as, for example, the explication of a concept in a purely expository syllogism should not by any means be belittled. Such a syllogism makes apparent an intelligibility which was already there. Progress herein does not so much come in visible steps (even though we may prefer to exhibit it in this form) as in degrees of awareness of an already present reality. The doctrine of the mystical body of Christ, for example, once established in the warp and woof of the divine plan (as described, say, in the Epistle to the Ephesians), is not built up from a series of "proofs" and links of cause and effect but as it were by extracting the kernel of its content and implications—such implications as the unity of the body and diversity of members, the effect of grace in individuals and in the body corporate, the presence of the Holy Spirit in the sacraments and in the Church, the Church's existence in time and in eternity, and so forth.

Or consider the virtue of hope. I shall gain a far better understanding of this by bringing to light the dynamic laws of the kingdom of God fulfilling themselves, individually and collectively, in a Church which looks toward the final revelation of Christ's second coming than by any *a priori* deductions about the state of the blessed in heaven. The introduction of rational categories will build up and maintain this understanding; and although discussions about the formal object and grounds of hope (variously described as God's generosity, his strength to help, or his trustworthiness) may give rise to speculations far removed from both the concrete and metaphorical promises of the Gospels, the sum total of such reasonings—about the basis of hope, its objects, motives, and the psychological analysis of hope as an emotion—do throw valid light on the historic fact of the divine promise which is now in the course of being fulfilled.

Certain trains of reasoning take the form of constructive analyses whose results do indeed go beyond the initial data but do not, however copious they may be, quite succeed in meeting all their own demands. One of the best examples is to be found in the theology of the gifts of the Holy Spirit. For a long time faith in grace as a participation in the divine life was expounded in a twofold doctrine of the necessary theological virtues and the presence of the Holy Spirit within the soul. This theology already goes deep into the heart of the matter, but a closer attention to the experience of the saints (and of simple believers too), together with a more flexible analysis of the suppleness needed in mental self-mastery (even on the natural plane, where St Thomas derived astonishing light from Aristotle), led the theologians further. The theological virtues may be strictly necessary to raise us to the level of the supernatural goal, but there are other and equally needful factors as well. There is a gap between the theological virtues and the spontaneity needed for a participation in the divine life, not because the virtues are inadequate but because we are unable to take full advantage of them without the promptings of the Holy Spirit—those supremely subtle, swift and freely-given promptings of which the rigid practice of virtue in this world takes no account. The logical demonstration of this would be laborious, but in the intimate understanding which experience brings we can gain a full and harmonious insight into the laws of the perfection of grace.

We may find an analogous instance in the manner in which theology gradually discerned, even in the compact vocabulary of the Holy Scriptures, the nature of, and the part played by, *charismata*—those special graces given to certain people, not for their own sanctification but for the general benefit of the Church. The whole history of the Church, not merely the exceptional period of her foundation, shows that the presence of these *charismata* is an essential fact in her constitution and her action. At the time when individualism was the prevailing mood in both religious and profane minds it seemed for a while as if these manifestations of the Spirit might be treated as merely an accessory, or even as suspect. Not long ago it was thought that they might well disappear without serious loss to the Church. Today, however, our faith has come to understand these gifts—through the experience of the expanding Church, the awakening of community feeling, the revival of the theology of the Fathers and a certain apostolico-prophetic mood in this restless modern world. These gifts are not so much those which involve an element of the miraculous but those which perform some vital function in the development of the mystical body of Christ (cf. the encyclical *Mystici corporis*) or which, in individuals, proclaims the mystical aspect in the moral plenitude of grace.

Finally, there are trains of reasoning whose object is to discover, by a process of deduction and, in principle, of demonstration, a middle term for the better understanding of the revealed datum. This may start from a definition and lead to a necessary property (for example, the Eucharist is a sacrament, therefore it must include a perceptible matter) or it may arrive at a definition by starting from an article of faith (for example, at a definition of "person" which, by modifying the philosopher's definition, would satisfy our faith in the Father, the Son and the Holy Ghost).

The introduction of a middle term, to the extent that it is given full play, forms a true demonstration whereby a third truth emerges from two foregoing truths—a creative operation of knowledge in which our intelligence discovers necessary links in the nature of things and obtains a complete explanation of their properties. It is not to be expected that such a high ideal, in which Greek rationalism excelled, should be achieved in every article of St Thomas' *Summa*; his subject-matter does not permit it, nor does the spiritual life demand it. Even if the deductive form of reasoning is found there, which does not happen very often, it must always take this necessary syllogistic form which is the mark of science. Arguments of this sort do exist, however, and may be placed in two categories:

first, arguments relating to the knowledge of God in which, assuming the existence of God, we can deduce the attributes which must belong to such a being, such as unity, goodness, omnipotence, etc.; and secondly arguments which are concerned with contingent realities in the plan of salvation, such as the humanity of Christ, the sacraments, or the society of the Church. Now in theological deduction there appear historical propositions stating contingent facts, and in such cases there cannot be a demonstration in the strict Aristotelian sense of the word; but once the facts have been admitted their truth carries implications whose inner necessity compels assent. If Christ was truly a man I can demonstrate that he had a human soul, that he acquired and used human science, that he experienced emotions, etc. From this enumeration alone it can be appreciated how ticklish such demonstrations are, not only because, in the history of Christian thought, they were not achieved without controversy and error (all of them have provoked heresies) but also because each one of the truths thus acquired has to be absorbed into the heart of the mystery— and, once there, they can no longer be treated as belonging to the everyday world. None of them can be regarded as merely one particular instance of a general rule. Christ did experience emotions—desire, sadness, hope; but these emotions, despite the free rein given them by the fact of their being "human", were subject to the presence and the control of his divine personality. The mystery of his agony is unfathomable by our human minds. Christ as a man did of course have a human conscience, but by this we must understand a conscience raised to his own level. Recent controversies have shown the subtlety of this problem. Let us say, in the language of the logician, that the rational middle term should be controlled and as it were internally transposed and extended beyond the range of its normal usage before it can take its place in *sacred* knowledge. I should be unable to accept the statement that God was made man and assumed the attributes of a man, nor admit the consequences of this, were it not for this control and this "transubstantiation". I should only credit a sacrament with all the attributes of its symbolism *within* the dogmatic concept of a sacrament and according to the exacting rules of analogy. For over the intellectual tools of his trade the theologian exercises a "divine right" which ensures his freedom in the use of his reasoning powers in the very act of using them.

To sum up: in the theological realism of faith, as in the absolute reality of God with whom he is in communion, the theologian does not dwell (as the philosopher with his syllogisms dwells) in a world of abstractions. He passes from the abstract to the concrete, and a logical purist would say that his middle term, which binds the major to the minor, has lost its identity. In the major we have an exact but jejune abstraction whose definition is supposed to be exhaustive; for example, "an individual substance of a rational nature" defines a "person"—that is, it includes all the characteristics which we attribute to the word. But in the minor premise the middle term takes on all the richness of a reality perceived in faith and expressed in the language of the Scriptures or of doctrine. Thus when we say, in the minor, that the Father or the Son is a "person" we are borrowing from the Scriptures or from tradition—that is, from a current, living, human language—a complex notion full of associations and nuances, enriched by our own experiences, coloured by our emotions and by analogies drawn from what we feel about the fellow-men whom we see and love. Doubtless this concrete, anthropomorphic image includes, in an eminent degree, the concept which the intellect abstracts from it, but the fact remains that the two are not identical. What connects two unequally abstract concepts is *analogy*—that major link which is the key to a whole method—and herein lies the distinctive characteristic of the theological syllogism. It resembles a geometrical syllogism which starts with perfect figures, rigid and void, generated in a homogeneous space by the movement of points and lines, and then takes a sudden leap into the realm of full and vivid forms, coloured, moving and varied, which constitute the actual furniture of the real, extended world. Again, in the reversal of the syllogism, where the generalized abstract definition is the product of deduction, the theological believer gives real content to the newly constructed concept. When we read that the object of hope is "eternal beatitude in the attainment of the supreme goal" we do not content ourselves with these abstract terms, however rational and clear they may be; we include them in the concrete and metaphorical tenets of our scriptural faith in the kingdom of God at work on earth according to the divine promise fulfilled in Christ.

Thus the purified concepts which we use to describe what is divine repay in purity and intelligibility what they lost for us in empirical precision. This in fact is what spiritual writers maintain: from the moment the soul frees herself from imaginary representations, the elements of the faith, so far from being empty abstractions, become for that soul an inexhaustible well of knowledge. "So soon as the mind has broken free from sensible images of material things it dwells in this pure and simple light. . . . For this light is always ready to shine in the soul. The images of created things presented by the imagination set up a resistance to this light, but it never fails to shine when all obstacles to it are removed."[3] Thus the theologian, in his syllogistic deductions, is constantly using his faith as a living filter. If he starts with rational and abstract definitions he ends up with individual, concrete attempts enriched by his own experience; and if, conversely, his deductions lead to concepts that appear to be more abstract, the light of faith will illumine them, just as it illumines the object of contemplative prayer.

Instead of finding a dry uniformity in theological reasonings we should rather observe their diversity and depth. Instead of seeing only dullness in their logical structure we ought rather to discern the intelligibility and certitude which lie beneath—

[3] St John of the Cross, *Ascent of Mount Carmel.*

as exemplified by the two main types of demonstration: proof by the cause and proof from the effects. Thus the proof of the immortality of the human soul has neither the same structure and tone, nor is it supported by the same evidence as the proof of the consubstantial union between soul and body. This is borne out by the fact that the two arguments play opposite parts in the original Aristotelian philosophy, which approves the latter but makes objections against the former. The dialectic of beatitude set forth several times by St Thomas (*Contra Gentiles*, II, 25–48; *Summa*, Ia, IIae, qu. 2, art. 1–8) is developed along very different lines and based upon very different foundations from those upon which he builds his five proofs of God's existence. The transcendental analysis of truth and goodness cannot be reduced to any single formal syllogism.

No less important is it to look at the foundations on which these premises rest, particularly the major. They often draw their intelligibility from acts of intellectual choice which are partly unconscious, and occasionally from certain "axioms" (cf. *infra*). Thus the intellectualist or voluntarist theses about beatitude, or about the nature of a human act, may rest upon a conventional demonstration; but in fact, deep down, they imply a conception of the mind, or an instinctive notion of human action, from which the major premise does gain "light from the depths" but which render it impervious to all opposing arguments. Not to take account of these underlying resources amounts to condemning oneself to see no more than the husk of the proof, and not its inner light.

If it be true that the whole force of a demonstration consists in the discovery of the *propria causa* based on "proper" principles (Aristotle, *I Post. Anal.*, 2, 71b, 9–11) the theologian must apply himself to following this clue. But such an ideal pattern is rare, and more often the working-out of a demonstration will be spread over several arguments, touch many different aspects of the objects in question and develop either by simple juxtaposition or by convergence. We must then establish both the independent validity of the arguments and their interaction by an exact determination of their starting-point.

Among the various forms of reasoning there is another type of discursive thought whose internal structure, as opposed to that of demonstration, gives it an altogether unique position—in theology more than in any other discipline. "Demonstration" is built up from *deductio*: we analyse a subject and derive a predicate from it because the predicate is contained in the subject. The converse process works backward from the content of a subject to its necessary presuppositions—to the conditions which render it intelligible—by a *reductio* which thus reveals implications of a quite different order. It is a *resolutio* in the strictly technical sense—by which thought, having grasped the complex, rediscovers the simple, even to the contemplation of simple existence. This dialectic, at the summit of a metaphysic of "participation", can indeed be expressed syllogistically, but in practice the movement of the mind is more straightforward and more concentrated. We reach a point where the intelligence functions, formally, as if it were itself transcendent and no longer like reason alone.

The principal instance of this, in philosophy and theology alike, is clearly the chapter which deals with the transcendental, towards which this "reduction" leads us and for which it provides the right analytic instrument—for example, the dialectic of Being and Oneness, the implications of the True and the Good, etc. Out of this "reflexive" metaphysic theologians of the Platonic type, like Meister Eckhart, draw with delight from sources that are often abstruse, and their work is consequently described as speculative mysticism; but it is far from being totally absent even from the works of St Thomas or St Bonaventure.

The dialectic of human action is also clarified by this same process of *re-solutio* in the depths of the human will. The will pursues its immediate ends by virtue of one supreme end, so that particular goods take their value within this universal will, and it, through them, leads us on to happiness. The slightest action, with its own particular end, is filled (both in the conceptual and the real order) by the selfsame will which brings us to the absolute, and therein lies the measure of its moral vitality. Satisfaction in the love of one particular good—condemned by the Jansenists as a *cupiditas* divorced from the love of the universal will—finds its vindication and its purification in this internal "reduction", in this plunging into depths below what is concretely determined. This contrast between Jansenist and Thomist ethics shows that the problem, although it starts as a philosophical one, soon takes on a religious dimension. We see that once again, beneath the theoretical surface, we are faced with alternatives that are spiritual. Theology issues commandments.

The most noteworthy example of this reductive analysis is that of the five "ways" by which St Thomas proves the existence of God, starting from metaphysical facts—becoming, causality, contingency, etc.—and ultimately ariving at pure Being. The whole dialectic of essence and existence (the two being distinct in the creature and constituting his ontological deficiency, whereas they are united in God who is the *Ipsum Esse*) develops according to the technique and in the atmosphere of this *resolutio*. Incidentally, this reveals how different, technically and spiritually, are the God of Aristotle and the God of St Thomas. Aristotle's Prime Mover is ontologically absent from the rest of the universe. The Thomist *Ipsum Esse* is shown to be present by the very deficiency of created beings. The intellectual *resolutio* involves a religious act which should never be hidden behind rational scaffolding. Dialectic and contemplation here dwell happily together in a single lofty experience.

This *reductio*, even in its psychological aspect, favours the introspective style and the sense of striving for the unattainable which we associate with contemplation. "This process is unusual from another aspect: it is a journey which never quite reaches its destination. It is forever having to begin again, and it is never more truly itself than when it fills us with the conviction both of its necessity and of its inevitable imperfection. It is a road whereon we set forth but which will never, this side of the grave, lead us to the resting-place of fulfilment and possession."[4] This could not be better expressed; nor can we ever too much insist on the way this ratiocination has its home *within* the mystery.

History, the history of western theology as well as that of Greek philosophy, reveals to what extent this process of *resolutio* (or *reductio*) is linked to neo-Platonism, and that too in its most thoroughgoing forms, the forms least acceptable to Christian doctrine. Scotus Erigena, the great neo-Platonist of the west (d. 875) who practised it as if it were as essential as definition, was always looked at with suspicion. St Thomas criticizes the vague use of the *via resolutoria* of the Jewish philosopher Ibn Gebirol. Eckhart, wrongly accused of pantheism by those who do not understand him, nevertheless misuses this method to the extent of building a metaphysical theology in which Christ no longer holds his proper place. Its very richness renders this method of returning to the Absolute One ill-suited to the contingencies and simplicities of the Gospel. Once again we see that the systems cannot monopolize all the treasures which they exploit, nor even their methods. For *resolutio*, the very soul and fine art of a return to God (or, if you like, of a quest for the Absolute) is not linked to the dialectic of ideas. It is the method of transcendental reflection—even in a realist philosophy where an awareness of concrete things can sustain the loftiest contemplation because the transcendental is recognized in the world of temporal Becoming. Yet it was not Plotinus nor Aristotle, it was St Thomas who was destined to make of it one of the most intimately personal parts of his methodology.

In any case this "resolution", by virtue of its object and its method, cannot fail to be a prototype of the divinely revealed science. Theology as a science is discursive; but to a greater

[4] L. B. Geiger, *La participation dans la philosophie de St Thomas* (Paris, 1942), p. 355.

extent than other sciences does it yearn for understanding. Starting from faith, as from the understanding of God, it does not rest until it returns there once again, bringing with it all that it has absorbed and elaborated. This is *resolutio* ordered and guaranteed by that communion which faith grants to it at its setting forth and which, in the mystery, gives us "the substance of things hoped for". Theology, in fact, seeks the knowledge of its conclusions only that it may the better understand its own first principles.

It is the same Platonic taste and style which governs the theologians' use of axioms. If it be true that the intellectual profundity of an argument originates in the major premise, or at least in the principle to which it refers all the steps of its progress, then particular interest will attach to those reasonings which are entirely subordinate to and as it were enveloped by very general judgements—judgements which cannot in the last resort be proved but which are accepted for their intrinsic lucidity and because their abstract and authoritative formulation gives a foretaste of their scope and intellectual value. With the masters these axioms sometimes lend as much life and strength to their main texts as to the general perspective of their systems. The following are among the more abstract examples: "In a given series, the primary member of a kind is the cause of all others of that kind" (*Primus in unoquoque genere est causa omnium illius generis*). "Agents are mutually subordinated in proportion to their purposes" (*Ordo agentium respondet ordini finium*).

These statements, propounded in isolation, waver between the pure theorem—wholly bound up with the inner coherence of an entire system of thought—and the platitude which exhibits more verbal profundity than scientific usefulness. "The character of what is received varies with the recipient" (*Quidquid recipitur ad modum recipientis recipitur*): for neo-Platonists, in the explanation of cosmic Becoming, this was a fundamental law of "participation"; but it can also be a vague, common-sense statement applying to every type of recipient. We must therefore tread delicately in our treatment of axioms, and all the more so because we need to determine their meaning not as we do in the case of a term to be defined but as we do in the case of a judgement. The meaning of a term can be established by reference to other terms through which it can be given a place in conventional vocabulary, but a proposition expresses an act of judgement, involving intelligence. This involvement can be treated as a hypothetical necessity where a proposition of this sort is needed to initiate any given demonstration (this is the modern usage of the word "axiom", as in the *ex suppositione* arguments of the Scholastics), but it can also be categorical, in spite of the fact that the proposition in question cannot be proved, and in that case it will be integral to a whole complex of perceptions which control a theological "system".

"Grace does not overthrow nature but perfects it" (*Gratia non tollit naturam, sed perficit*). This is a famous aphorism of St Thomas; nowhere does he undertake to prove its truth; but this generalization, derived from induction and applied as a principle, undoubtedly governs his thought at its deepest and most intimate levels. As we have seen, he uses it to establish the competence of faith, trusting in reason, to construct a theology wherein the distinction between nature and grace shall not disturb the religious homogeneity of our knowledge.

Many of these axioms in medieval theology have an obviously Platonist origin and colour. It is in the wider perspective of a system—the Dionysian system, for instance—that they find their natural place. Their use certainly has some objective value, but in order to avoid ambiguity it is necessary to set forth the underlying motive for using them and to indicate the particular points upon which they are going to bear. Compare some of St Thomas's better-constructed articles and several passages in St Bonaventure's *Itinerarium mentis*.

This axiom-building has always had, and still has, a curious fascination for the mathematically-minded. Men of this sort, when they apply themselves to theology, seek to organize the corpus of revealed truth in a series of rigidly linked ideas, like theorems, whose sheer conciseness seems to bring in its train a mysterious intelligibility. "God is an intelligible sphere whose centre is everywhere and whose circumference is nowhere" (*Deus est sphaera intelligibilis, cuius centrum ubique, circumferentia nusquam*). This formula, later made famous by Pascal, is one of the happier examples out of a collection of twenty-four twelfth-century aphorisms whose aim was to describe divinity. It was taken up by Alain of Lille (d. 1204) in an essay which is the most perfect attempt ever made to construct a Christian theology *more geometrico* and which begins with the primary axiom, *Monas est qua quaelibet res est una* ("A monad is that in virtue of which any object is one"). The attempt was doomed to failure; but it did at least show, as in the Greek Hermetic cult to which it looks back, a significant conjunction of mystic sensibility with the most rational abstraction.

In all the modes of reasoning so far discussed we have made repeated reference to the logic and epistemology of the Greeks, as presented by Plato, Aristotle or their successors; and it is a fact that western theology does trace its ancestry to the rationalism and methods of the ancient Greeks. Theology as such, however, concerned as it is with the transcendent Word of God, is not confined to the use of these methods alone. Since it has also a scriptural ancestry it is equally at home among categories, procedures, modes of thought and literary genres which derive from the very different culture of the Semites and which, for the expression of certain religious truths, occupy a position of privilege. M. Massignon in particular has given a high place to the richness of the Semitic language; and without setting up a biblical metaphysic in opposition to Greek philosophy we may admit that the transcendence of God, the creation, and the predicament of mankind are not so homogeneously and spontaneously expressed in the Hellenic categories as they are in the Scriptures.

The human reason, in its fundamental purposes, is immutable and universal; but its scope is elastic and not all its resources of form and method were exhausted by the Greco-Latin culture. Some remained to be exploited beneath other skies. Did not Dionysius describe contemplation in terms of "straight, circular and spiral tracks", using an imagery which already goes beyond the *schemata* of Aristotelian logic? Quite recently the spiritual energy of the human understanding among the Bantu peoples has been brought to light, and nobody doubts that the mind of the Hindus has the power to mobilize, one day, powerful forces for the expression of the faith which would be quite foreign to European ways of thought. The remarkable success of western scholasticism does not condemn theology to imprisonment within its boundaries. The faith's transcendence joins with the infinite resources of the mind, and both are ready to receive the light of God.

ARGUMENTS FROM FITTINGNESS

Although the theologian may consent (in extreme humility combining faith with reason) to bring his understanding of certain inner coherences within the mystery to the pitch of demonstrative proof, it remains true that his original data, so far as God's own initiatives are concerned, are not themselves amenable to such demonstration. That God created the world, that in the world he placed a creature made in his own image and that in order to restore that image in mankind he took the way of incarnation—these are facts that can never be rationally demonstrated. They spring from love, and from love's irrationality. The best that reason can do with this divine revelation is to contemplate and admire the harmony of the design so revealed. Reason may still discuss, but her arguments will have no compulsive force. To describe this task the theologians use a characteristic phrase: such arguments are "arguments from fittingness".

Aristotelian epistemology objects to such arguments on the

ground that they cannot reach that perfect intelligibility which Aristotelians demand; but whereas the latter cannot reconcile themselves to such "probable" knowledge the theologians, on the contrary, find this realm highly congenial to them. Here they find reason and mystery conjoined in one programme and one operation which fully satisfies their need for an "understanding" which can be combined with love and adoration. The reality and the actions of God cannot be bounded by the categories of logic. For example: why did not the incarnation of the Word of God take place immediately after the fall of man? Because revelation is a sort of pedagogy, and as such it had to move step by step. The natural order of things (and of the mind) is to move from the imperfect to the perfect, and so Christ must come after a long period in which the people of God are made ready for him. The principle is sound, in the sense that the realization of any plan involves a previous preparation of the elements concerned; but its application to a given chronology is far from self-evident. God has the power, if he chooses, to adapt imperfect elements to his plan instantaneously. The application of the principle can certainly be justified historically, and the facts of history will regulate my faith; but in the form which the theologians give to it the argument is only a dialectical proof which cannot, in the abstract, compel assent.

Other examples: it was in the highest degree fitting that the mother of God-made-man should be exempt from the stain of original sin. It was in the highest degree fitting that her flesh should be exempt from corruption and that her body should achieve, before all others, that resurrection which her Son had earned. These famous arguments, whose growing ascendancy during the course of centuries is so significant of the faith's inner laws of development, exhibit the efficacy of that "fittingness" where in the believer's piety (in the deepest sense of the word) delights. They already hint at truths of doctrine which were for a long time hidden in the womb of the Church. They are not decisive or demonstrative arguments but they give pregnant expression to an authentic understanding of God's design and of the ways in which he brought it to pass. These instances are, of course, the major ones. The history of theology includes many others which, without in any sense approaching dogmatic ratification, do have great value in the nourishment they give both to truth and fervour. In his treatise on the Incarnation St Thomas attaches great importance to a "theological" reading of the Gospels and the life of Christ; each episode is illustrated by a "fittingness" which in no way aspires to be a proof but which manifests what one may call the divine "inwardness" of the facts. It is a pity that a tendency towards intellectualist positivism has sometimes caused these meditations of the ancient theologians to be neglected.

This sort of research has for its direct subject-matter the fundamental teachings of the Church. That the living God is one, in three persons of the Father, Son and Spirit, is something I can only know by faith. Alleged "presentiments" of this truth in the writings of pagan philosophers are only the effect of vague and rather far-fetched analogies—thus, "a perfect being will be self-reproducing" or "a perfect life involves personal relationships" or even, in the *mystique* of numbers, "three is a perfect and sacred number". But these premonitions do find, in the light of faith, a strange verification; they become intelligible and valid in a manner unsuspected by the philosopher. St Thomas goes so far as to say that in such *ex post facto* verification we reach "the roots of truth" (*Summa*, Ia, qu. 32, art. 1, resp. 2). St Anselm spoke of "necessary reasons" and Richard of St Victor of the exaltation of his spirit by "proving" that, in its fullness, love is self-reproducing. Expressions like these must, of course, be weighed in the balance, but their splendid optimism marks the thorough-bred theologian.

There is another and very exalted part played by this kind of argument in the world of theology, namely, the choice which it leads a theologian to make in the architectural or schematic construction of his synthesis—in his "Summa", as they called it in the Middle Ages. If in my working out of the data of revelation I arrange all the elements so as to centre them upon the incarnation and make all other truths depend upon this divine act, my conspectus will clearly be very different from that of St Thomas, who organizes his own *Summa* on the basis of the neoplatonic *schema* of emanation and return—so that the historical fact of the incarnation is simply the means taken to accomplish, in Christ, man's return to God. No proof is offered of this or that disposition of the data; neither does the intelligibility of a theological system, however decisive it may be as regards its originality, arise from any article of faith. One and the same faith inspires the systems of Hugh of St Victor, Bonaventure, Thomas Aquinas and Duns Scotus. But this underlying orthodoxy leaves the theologian completely at liberty to make a personal choice of the axis, so to speak, about which to construct and organize his rational "Summa". For theology, though derived from faith, is nevertheless explicitly distinguished from faith itself. There is no necessary connection between faith and what a theologian may choose to consider "fitting".

NON-RATIONAL FUNCTIONS

Despite the care we have taken to take account of all the various procedures which reason employs to elaborate the content of the faith we cannot but admit that in the field of theology some mental resources come into play which are non-rational—or which can at least only in part be reduced to rational form. If we were to enlarge, as we should like to enlarge, the frontiers of theology so as to include those thoughts about the faith which are not derived from instruction, cate-chesis, or theology in the usual sense of the word, we should come upon certain byways of thought, originating in the imagi-nation, which nourish and sometimes profoundly instruct our faith. Their themes can indeed be turned into "reasons", but within and beyond such reasons they conceal a value and power which it would be a pity to neglect. For example,

tians, to treat these spiritual jewels as childish playthings. Some departments of theology are particularly well adapted to exploit these non-rational processes, not only in the psychological sphere but also in that of doctrine, and especially in that frontier-region between mystery and rationality where the inadequacy of reason is specially felt. The mystics know this well. They have recourse to imagery, even to poetry. Dionysius (their master in this, as in so much else) holds that of two infirmities in the spirits of earth-bound men the symbol is a medium more apt than the rational concept with which to express the mystery. The symbol may indeed be brought low by the gross weight of our senses, but the concept may lead us into the illusions of idealism.

In the Christian economy there is one whole region concerned with symbols and their use—not only verbal symbols but symbols in action—namely, the actions and representations which we call sacramental; starting with the seven basic sacraments but including also the whole network of cult-actions, all those "celebrations" which form the warp and woof of the liturgy, expressing individually or socially the mystery of Christ. Mystery and sacrament are complementary; indeed, the two words are at times actually synonymous, for we speak of the sacrament of the Eucharist as a celebration of the "sacred mystery". The significance of this lies in the fact that we give to external actions a meaning which is not only sacred but Christian. The sacraments are essentially signs; and not merely abstract or theoretical signs but signs that are sensible and material (a bath of water, a meal, etc.). We might say, with the theologians of the eastern Church, that they are symbols with a special representational potency. The Catholics had to defend against Luther the reality of the inward grace of which the sacrament was the outward sign, but, granted that dogmatic truth, it remains true that the sacrament is also a symbolic representation of what it signifies and of what it brings to pass. Thus a rich liturgy allows full play to the symbols—words and gestures—which it employs. The condition of its efficacy (as we see today in the present liturgical reawakening, in the revival of the Easter vigil) is the refinement of a spiritual sensibility educated by symbolic expression, according to its own laws and according to the aptitude of the participants. If, moreover, we recall that the liturgy is one of the living sources of theology, one of its "homes", as it were, we may assess how much the symbolic and sacramental expression of the revelation can nourish from within our appreciation of the faith.

A second department of the Christian faith appeals to symbolic representations in a manner quite different from the foregoing. God's plan in the history of our salvation evolves not only in a sequence of events—from the call of Abraham to the resurrection of Christ; from the coming of the Holy Spirit to the return of Christ—but in a typological series of stages wherein facts and deeds have in addition to their own reality a special value as representations of what is to come. Jerusalem was the holy city of the Jews; but it was also a prefiguration of the Church, and finally it is a type of the celestial city of God. The manna was a holy food for the people of God; but if it retains any theological interest it is rather as a figure of the Eucharist or even of the banquet of heaven, and so on. Theological history is full of such symbolic elaborations, within the fabric of the revelation itself. The Fathers, both in their sermons and in their writings, continually nourish their *intellectus fidei* with such symbolism. The great scholastic masters, devoted as they were to conceptual and "scientific" values, still preserve and exploit this traditional method. St Thomas who, as we shall see, excludes it from the strictly scientific function of theology, nevertheless has recourse to it on an extensive scale in those long sections of the *Summa* which are devoted to the theology of the Old Law—as also in those concerned with the text of the liturgy.

St Thomas's reason for excluding symbolism from the scope of scientific theology was that among his contemporaries there had arisen a curious attempt to build a whole theology upon a purely symbolist basis. Hugh of St Victor (d. 1141) had planned, and his disciples endeavoured to realize, a vast programme of work which should first inventory all the data of revelation and then seek to understand them by rational means —starting from a grammatical and historical exegesis of Scripture and finally working out a systematic structure of arguments. But all this was to be mere groundwork, a bringing of the Word of God into the field of study. The next step was to be the construction of a theological edifice no longer built with "reasons" but with organized symbols and allegory. Allegory in fact, in its traditional context, exactly fulfilled the function of a doctrinal interpretation of Scripture, enabling the faithful to penetrate into the inner spiritual meaning of the sacred texts. Important as it was to preserve the letter of the text as a foundation, it was equally important to allegorize it so as to nourish and build up our faith. "The letter teaches us the facts, allegory the content of our faith" (*Littera gesta docet, quid credas allegoria*), ran the accepted axiom. Thus were history and faith systematically buttressed—faith gave understanding of the "mysteries" of history, history set forth the material of revelation. Hugh of St Victor essayed to construct the whole Word of God into a system along these lines. Thus the temple, whose architecture and functions are described in the *letter* of the Bible, becomes in the eyes of a "theological" reader the figure (and a figure inexhaustible, devotionally and intellectually) of the Church, the soul and finally of the celestial city. Here is a threefold allegorization which deals with the scriptural material organically, not in the maundering, imaginative manner of certain pious interpreters. Similarly the Exodus, a great spiritual theme, is more than a bare episode in primitive history: the passage through the wilderness into the promised land and its celebration in the ritual of the Passover are a true type of the institution of the people of God. The Passover of Christ and the Christian Easter find therein not only the archaeological context of an otherwise obscure liturgy but a primary image which illuminates with a single ray of light the creation, nature, sacrifice, resurrection, Eucharist and finally the promised land of paradise. So with the sacrifice of the paschal lamb. So with the Sabbath. So with everything else. Without going any further we can recognize in all this the recurring themes of catechesis and pastoral preaching. How could the academic theologian be oblivious of them?

This, said Hugh of St Victor, is the way of an understanding reader—the *iter-legendi*—if it be true that the Bible is something more than a sequence of narratives and statements and is a systematic structure of divine thought. The strictly rational working out of the revelation (what we today would call speculative theology) is thus treated as only a necessary prelude, allied with the grammatical interpretation of the text. Hugh did in fact compose a *Summa* but it was intended to be, pedagogically and methodologically, a mere preliminary to that "allegorical" study whose construction was the theologian's supreme duty and the only true abode of mystical understanding properly so called.

His attempt, at least in its original design, was not destined to come to fruition; but it was highly significant, and we have not cited it as a by-way of scholarship. Hugh was right to regard the typological aspect of Holy Scripture as essential to an understanding of the plan of salvation. What is more, the theologian, on pain of converting that plan into an abstract system and emptying it of all historical content, must integrate his *doctrina sacra* with that divine dynamism which links remembrance of things past and intimations of final ends for the benefit of the here and now. Indeed, every time the Church experiences an evangelical re-awakening—with all its exegetical, doctrinal and pastoral demands—such as we are witnessing at the present day, one of the proofs of its genuineness is the renewed fertility it brings to the spiritual significance of Scripture (without injury to the literal and historical meaning) which testifies to the active presence of the Word of God. And allegory in the Pauline sense (cf. Gal. 4. 24) is the mainspring of this understanding.

But allegory has its laws, and they are not the laws of conceptual analysis and rational synthesis. Dionysius had long since explicitly distinguished between these two highways of knowledge, and the application of Aristotelian method established this distinction more securely. Definitions, ideas and arguments cannot live happily alongside a "polysemantic" symbolism made up as it is of the stuff of imaginative and emotional associations. To build up a theological science and develop theological arguments by conceptualizing the types and symbols of the Scriptures is to mingle incompatibles. The result will be to corrupt both rationality and symbolism. The wretched products of allegorization, alike in the interpretation of Scripture and the explanation of ritual, reveal to us this vicious perversion of symbolism, which by its very nature is unamenable to such intellectualization. The symbols and the types are unquestionably part of the revealed truth, but theology, when it is exercising its scientific function, must exclude them from its field. This is the meaning of St Thomas's decision that the theologian may draw his arguments only from the literal sense of the Scriptures, not from what they teach by allegory. This is the way to unravel some of the confusions in the fervour of contemporaries, by according to each method its own rights in its own sphere.

"SACRED" SCIENCE

St Thomas offers us a justification of rational methods, taken to the point where this understanding of the faith can qualify as a true "science", which despite its technical character is well worth rehearsing here. It is true, as we have said, that some theologians of the first rank (even among Thomists) and some other schools of theology do not accept either the science or the justification; but freedom of opinion does not exempt us from the duty of getting to grips with the problem of which this is the crucial nexus. Theological science is only a science within

a mystical continuity with the Word of God. This, episte-
mologically, is the situation.

Theology is the science of God. It is so in a general sense
inasmuch as faith enables us to participate in God's own knowledge of himself. It is so in a more exact sense inasmuch as this
participated knowledge builds itself up within us in scientific
form. This holds good, says St Thomas, in spite of the following direct challenge to the very notion of a science, namely,
that theology, being the child of faith, can only exist in submission to the Word of God, in loyalty to its mysteries, in
obedience to its dogmas and consequently in the absence of
any evidence for its basic principles. But this very lack of
evidence is itself the reason why no scientific consistency is
conceivable without an organic continuity with the light of
God.

An anomalous state of affairs for a "science"? Not so. To be
sure, every science needs to be based on evidence; but the
scientist's independence and mental autonomy are not an
absolute, without degrees or variations, and the complex
organism of knowledge compels us to bend and mould this
principle to suit the scope of different disciplines. Truth is one,
but the truth within our minds is composed of divers systems
of truths, and none of these is obliged to find within itself
and on its own level the ultimate evidence for its ultimate
starting-points. Each system, at each level, forms part of some
higher system, just as the epistemological analysis of objects
themselves reveals divers stages of intelligibility included within
one another like Chinese boxes. Evidence of various kinds
dominates and illuminates each system and confers autonomy
upon it, but it is always evidence *within a given field*. Short of
erecting its existing knowledge into a supreme science (and
this is the besetting sin of the specialist) the mind reserves a
sort of discontent, an unsatisfied appetite, and if one day the
mind seeks to satisfy that appetite by going in quest of further
light, this will not affect adversely the originality and special
validity of the subordinate disciplines to which it has hitherto

been devoted. The physicist explores the intelligibility of his subject-matter by using principles and evidence borrowed from mathematics. He can, it is true, re-ascend the ladder and validate the arithmetical or geometric theorems upon which his own work depends, but if he stays on his own level he will accept from his mathematical partner those conclusions about numbers, surfaces and volumes which, applied on the plane of physics, provide him with adequate light and constitute "basic principles" for true knowledge; and that without any detriment to his own mind or his own subject-matter. The Physicist accepts these principles "on faith", but this does not corrupt them nor deter him from borrowing them. Mental discipline demands approval for this "hierarchy of evidences" because in recognizing such degrees of knowledge we recognize that there are degrees of intelligibility among beings. This methodological suppleness is characteristic of Aristotle's noetics and it is founded, in his own writings, not only upon a clear-sighted epistemology but upon a metaphysic of Being. The theory of the analogy of being is fundamental to this conception of knowing—multiplex in the autonomy of successive degrees despite the unity of the mind. The link between these intelligibilities is established by the "faith" whereby the sciences are subordinated one to another—that is, the "subalternation of the sciences", to use the more technical Latin term.

Thus the "submission" of the theologian who "believes" in his basic principles without possessing evidence for them is only one particular example of a normal scientific rule. The *faith* which provides him with his light and his mental atmosphere is analogous to the mental coordinates which define a scientist's field of study. And just as the physicist, his appetite whetted, seeks to raise himself from the level of his own first principles to the level of intelligibility of the mathematician, so the theologian, in the appetite of his faith, seeks a clear view of those divine truths which hitherto he has "believed". His science depends upon God's knowledge, or the knowledge of those who "see" God, and despite his intense hunger for such "seeing" he believes without hesitation the received truths and makes them the "principles" of theology.

The striking thing about this solution of the antinomy of "evidence-faith" is not the technical dexterity of the answer but its incorporation within the very warp and woof of the problem set. It is drawn from within—not by extending an originally inadequate thesis to cover an unforeseen contingency but by validating it out of that very conception of "science" which originally gave rise to the antinomy itself. Science, analysed in its structure and in the conditions under which it functions, now reveals a hidden harmony between itself and theology—a discipline of which Aristotle had never heard. The very thing which threatened to sever all contact is the one which on the contrary renders friendly relations secure—namely, the Aristotelian theory of science.

Thus both the technical demands of science and the religious sense as well combine to force theology to make faith its starting-point, to depend upon faith, since it is faith which ensures a continuity between the "Science of God" (subalternating) and theological science (subalternated). There follows not only the delivery of a datum, of a set of propositions accepted authoritatively by a legitimate intellectual "obedience" to a self-revealing God, but an organic, psychological and religious continuity wherein the light of faith—an emanation of the divine light in the mind of man—constitutes the indispensable *milieu* for the knowledge of what has been revealed.

Consequently the mystic who refuses to regard as true religious knowledge a rational dialectic dependent upon a non-believing acceptance of the articles of faith finds justification in this law of the subalternation of the sciences; for it insists that "continuity" within the hierarchy of mental disciplines is the essential condition of their validity and vitality. And the very factor which makes theology scientific is the one which makes it "sacred"—we would willingly say "mystical" if that venerable word had not become ambiguous. The theory of subordination is no more than the technical formulation of what is a structural necessity in theological knowledge.

And so, to wind up this justification, we can repeat and reconsider a sentence which might otherwise appear seriously ambiguous or inconsistent, namely, that in this continuity of light, in this communion of life, the theologian hears the Word of God and speaks the Word of God. He converses with God, and this converse, indissolubly linked with faith, confers upon theology its divine "existence".

The science of theology therefore took a very wrong turning when, under the influence of de Wolff's rationalism, some theologians (for a time, and more or less consciously) robbed theological knowledge of this impregnating light of faith and represented rational knowledge as self-supporting. As if arguments, deductions and proofs could have any validity without faith, without the continuity of faith in communion with the Word of God! In this academic optimism, which was the mental climate of the *Aufklärung* or Enlightenment, this pseudo-scientific theology did preserve dialectical correctness, but it lacked those perennial and inexhaustible wells of intelligibility—the power of contemplation and wide-ranging speculation—which were fostered by the unsophisticated faith of the medieval theologians. The "theodicy" of the deists was nothing but a series of theorems, lacking transcendence, spirituality and every attribute of religion—the religion of Voltaire. Today, a theological renaissance is leading us back from this decadent scholasticism.

In the structure of theological reasoning the mysteries of God do not constitute particular instances of some more general rule, as if they were the minor premise in a syllogism whose major was a general principle. We must at all costs eschew such arguments as: "A sacrifice is . . . (so-and-so, definition borrowed from the philosophy of religion). But Christ offered himself as a sacrifice. Therefore . . . (conclusion such-and-such)." Or again: "Priesthood is defined as so-and-so. But Christ is a priest. Therefore . . . etc." No. In Christ the sacrifice, priesthood, the entire Christian *fact* (Christological, anthropological, sacramental, ecclesiastical) must be considered as a thing preeminent, primordial, specific, incapable of being reduced to any common formula save by way of analogy, and always strictly regulated and as it were drenched by faith. Reasoning must never appear to be the application of philosophical notions to ordinary, heterogeneous material. There is a danger, not always avoided, "of regarding faith as no more than a preliminary—necessary to provide theology with a starting-point but still a mere prelude, external to the real work of the theologian which is simply to apply metaphysics to those data which have been accepted as true. But how then, while contriving a rational interpretation, can we preserve the unique character of the Christian revelation, its wholeness, its primary reality?"[6]

From end to end of its unique course theology is *doctrina sacra*. It works, to be sure, at different levels of intelligibility, and we must also explicitly distinguish within this sacred unity the revelation itself (which is the object of faith) from what the schoolmen called the "virtual" revelation which is the proper object of theological science. But this distinction implies no separation. At the end of his theory of subalternation St Thomas can say, in words which defy translation, that faith is *quasi habitus theologiae*.

THE EXAMPLE OF THE MIDDLE AGES

This lofty conception of a theological knowledge of God is to be found in the medieval universities in the thirteenth century, the "classical era" of theology. It affords us an example of a formula *in action*, exhibited to perfection not only in written texts but also in institutions and in the whole scholastic mode of teaching.

[6] M.-J. Congar, article on theology in the *Dictionnaire de théologie catholique*, col. 480.

Theological teaching in the Middle Ages was built up on three operations, at once distinct and interconnected. Distinct in-so-far as the student, as he advanced, had to make separate programmes of them, but connected in the sense that their close interdependence had to be respected even though the need for specialization caused them to be distinguished. Their Latin names deserve to be used, for they represent the technical product of a long period of active evolution. They were called *lectio, quaestio* and *disputatio*. *Lectio*, as its name implies, in theology as elsewhere, was a "reading" of texts and commentaries upon them—starting with the "letter" (grammar and logic), proceeding to the "sense" (extracted by a preliminary conceptualization) and thence to the message or doctrine (*sententia*) which went deeper than the text and was arrived at by a study of the interconnections and implications within the thought. In theology it was of course the Bible which was "read" at all levels and at every stage of a progressive programme, starting with a simple recitation and ending with a true biblical theology. This was the essential "course" in any theological instruction. Always and everywhere it held the first place, in dignity and method. Theology was literally biblical. The basic text for a master's degree in theology was the Bible. St Thomas, in his magisterial thesis, commented on the Bible.

The second operation was the *quaestio*. The story of this university exercise cannot be told in full, suggestive as it is, but it shows that the *quaestio* was the system's perfect fruit. On the basis of the text, after it had been read and understood, a question was put—and that in the strongest sense of "calling in question" the doctrine which the text contained. It might be a question about some obscurity in the text or a question about its consistency with the literary or doctrinal context, but soon it would become a question about the very content of the text. Arising at first spontaneously, as difficulties were encountered in the course of reading, this process of "challenge" soon became methodical. It became generalized into a technique in which the reader, spurred by curiosity and using the tools of dialectic, proposed artificial questions about each sentence—or at least about the more important points—in his text. It represents a vital step in theological progress and is typical of the scholastics' proprietorial attitude and manner of drawing up title-deeds. We see, as it were, a young man born into the life of the mind and coming of age when he "calls in question" those things which he had hitherto accepted passively. We have reached the maturity of reason in the west, including theological reason. Henceforth the professor is no longer an exegete solely; he is a "master" who, in the soon-to-be-accepted formula, "determines" the questions—not by citing authorities which (despite obedience and certainty) would leave the understanding still hungry, but by *reasons* which uncover the root of things to the inquiring mind. So speaks St Thomas (*Quodlibet*, IV, art. 18).

This is the precise point at which, within authority, including divine authority, reason steps in. This is "scholastic" theology. Every article in St Thomas's *Summa* is in form and substance a *quaestio*—a bringing into question. *Utrum*: is it yes, or is it no? The multiplication of questions and their intensification were no longer simply the normal reinforcement of the reading of the text. They implied a shift in the object itself, the object of curiosity and the object of the theologian's labour. Curiosity was no longer concerned with a textual problem to be solved in the simple light of faith but with a speculative, extra-Scriptural problem for which the Scriptures provided only the substratum and whose working out had nothing to do with exegesis and its grammatical or dialectical rules. We have passed from the *sacra pagina* to the *sacra doctrina*. The *sententia* has become the conclusion of a train of reasoning.

Disputatio. Here the question was, how to conduct an operation of this sort without giving rein to conflict of opinion, interference by presuppositions as to system and method and, in short, how to prevent discussion from turning into dispute. The "disputation" was a dispute conducted according to set rules and along officially recognized lines. The "question in dispute" became a school-exercise in which the master re-hearsed the arguments *pro* and *contra*, stated the principles whereby he proposed to resolve the question, applied them to diverse elements brought to light either by spoken controversy or careful study of a given text, and finally reached his so-called "determination"—that is, he closed the debate by giving his authorized *sententia*. This disputation became, by reason of its scope, difficulty and originality the special province of the Master of Theology. Roger Bacon complained that even in his day it was ousting the study and understanding of the Bible both from the theologian's lecture-hall and from public favour. However this may have been it is nevertheless clear in principle that the *disputatio magistralis* held great potentialities for an understanding of the faith and provided the mind with a tool well adapted to its use—at any rate in some realms of thought. The scholastic *quaestio* differs from the Socratic dialogue, the Cartesian doubt and the Hegelian dialectic. Even in the Middle Ages it left room for other methods, inductive and deductive. But it was none the less preponderant and, as the principal act in the *intellectus fidei*, it led to the formulation of the "article" as the unit in the various Summas.

The originality of this theological technique will be better appreciated if we compare it with the most common arrange-ment in present-day handbooks. In these the *schema* is set forth quite differently—not in "questions" but in "theses", supported by multiform proofs—scriptural, patristic or rational. In these the scientific functions of theology are juxtaposed to textual exegeses, the Bible is no longer treated as something to be read by the faithful for its own sake, and exegesis is no more than an auxiliary to the reasonings of the theologian. But *lectio, quaestio, disputatio*—the tripartite *schema* of the medieval scholastics was more skilful in preserving both the unity of theology and the diversity of its functions.

THE MASTER'S RÔLE

In a medieval university the gaining of a licentiate—*licentia docendi*—meant more than passing an examination. It conveyed the title of teacher and the right to teach. The licentiate in theology held a mandate to teach the Word of God, and the Church would uphold his teaching.

Once the scholastic system had, as we have seen, become fully developed, once the "reading" of the text had been followed by the "question," the theologian's official function tended to become split into two halves—the interpretation of the sacred texts on the one hand and a speculative and systematic elaboration of them on the other. Thus did the "masters" come into being as a sociological order within the Church who is the "mistress" in matters of faith and morals. She found in them not only experts and counsellors in her synods but also, in her day-to-day teaching, men qualified to give clear expression to the faith. They could not, of course, be reckoned among "authorities" (such as the Fathers, the canonized Doctors, the liturgy and the general consensus of Christian opinion) but they provided a reasoned and reasonable statement of the mysteries of faith within a framework of orthodoxy, and they worked out its rational implications and applications. An understanding of the faith now implied more than a rigidly orthodox adherence to the data of revelation; it implied a rational and coherent set of propositions borrowed from the philosophy of man and nature and employed as part of a logical system. Later on, theological assertions came to be called merely "opinions"; but that term does too little honour to the certitudes of theological science and to the part played in the Church by the "master of theology" in throwing positive light upon matters of faith. It also implies that faith, being a pure and unreasoning submission, will take no account of the reasons worked out by theologians and will regard them as merely adventitious curiosities intruding upon the monolithic integrity of faith. Well, St Thomas was a mere theologian.

But he was a theologian, and the Church has exalted him as such into the high places from which her thought derives.

The Church has also had recourse from time to time, in centuries gone by, not only to individual theologians but also to collective bodies of them. Intervention by the university of Paris in the Middle Ages, by the doctors of the Sorbonne under the old régime and by the theologians of Salamanca have become famous. It is well known that the Union of Freiburg in the time of Leo XIII prepared the material for his encyclical *Rerum novarum*. The Malines conversations laid the foundations of the ecumenical movement. In 1921 an international team of theologians, laymen and clergy, assembled at Malines and produced the "Social Code" dealing with the problems raised by social evolution in the nineteenth century. "Certain good men and true," as one eminent theologian recently declared, "desired to revive an ancient custom now falling into desuetude. The common opinion of theologians in any age, although it cannot furnish an absolute rule of orthodoxy, is nevertheless in a privileged sense a 'word of the Church'."[7]

The master of theology, moreover, is no mere "professor". Peter Cantor (d. 1197), who is a good witness to the appearance of these masters upon the scene, being himself a Master in the university of Paris, described their rôle in a celebrated formula. He defined it as a complete energizing of the Word of God: *legere* ("reading" in the sense described above), *disputare* (the working out of questions), and *predicare* (preaching). Three functions—differentiated but united in the *sacra doctrina* more profoundly than would ever be possible empirically. Their separation, as occasion may demand, in no way impairs their full and necessary unity within the unique Word of God. True mastery *in sacra pagina* belongs to preaching; the theology of the Word of God is not accomplished save in the handing-on of the message. And thus the great heralds of thirteenth-century evangelism, the chiefs of the companies of wandering teachers in those days—Robert of Arbrissel, Norbert of Magdeburg,

[7] Fr d'Ouince, *La Croix*, July 31st, 1957.

Dominic—are denominated "masters". Exegesis, dogmatics, evangelism—these three are the conjoined foundation-stones for any understanding of the Gospel, for this understanding can only be brought to full realization in the active proclamation of the Word.[8]

The status of the theologian in the Church, on the personal plane, is the same as that of theological science itself on the institutional plane in a Church empowered by Christ to preserve, transmit and develop the deposit of faith. Theology, theological science and theologians are necessary to the Church. Her authority, far from being diminished by their specialized activities, finds therein a source of nourishment—a green pasture. *Fides quaerens intellectum.* To pursue this quest, to slake this thirst, in the realms of reason is to win for the faithful an understanding which will enable them to walk, not empty-headed, in the paths of full obedience to the Word of God and to his Church (cf. St Thomas, *Quodlibet*, IV, art. 18).

[8] Thus some thirteenth-century masters (Henry of Ghent), conscious of the link between the message of faith and the science of theology, discussed the question of how far theology can be transmitted by instruction alone. A noble question!

CHAPTER V

THEOLOGICAL SYSTEMS

Most of the great theologians have one trait in common which enables us to appreciate and appraise one final effect of their science: they reach the point where they build it into a "system"—that is, a logical whole, planned architecturally, wherein the various elements are so disposed as to knit together and buttress the entire structure.

Systematization is a normal and proper consequence of a rational understanding of the faith. By achieving that unity which the human mind perennially demands and needs, it consummates the efforts of reason. Yet it seems appropriate to devote a separate chapter, apart from the consideration of theological science as such, to this final task of the theologians. Not that all of them have in fact reached this point. Many Doctors of the Church, deep and authoritative thinkers though they were, chose not to express their thought systematically at all. Their temperament, genius, or the fashion of their personal faith, disinclined them to construct their understanding of the faith in this shape. St Augustine did not built a *summa*. St Anselm, rationalist as he was, did not express his mastery of the subject in this form. Some, lingering nearer to the revelation itself, preferred a more meditative approach to the heart of it. Others expressed themselves in language so lofty as almost to reach the borderland of poetry.

There is another and more specific reason why we draw this distinction between science and system in theology. The disjunction is admittedly an arbitrary one—to separate in the fabric of a theological "summa" the thread which relates to scientific elaboration from that which adds to it a systematic construction. It is on the contrary from their systematic selections that their theological science takes its colour. And here again we recognize how theological reasoning is the happy effect of the contemplative power of faith. When St Thomas laid down the original, very original, plan of his *Summa* the process was not secondary to his main purpose, not a mere marshalling of his material; it was the effect of a single vision of the totality, and every detail of the work is saturated by his original conspectus of the whole.

If, then, we do distinguish science and system it is with reference to epistemological criteria in accordance with which we mark out on the one hand those conclusions reached by theological reasoning whose certainty is acceptable to all and, on the other hand, those decisions which, made at the deepest level of personal meditation, cannot be rendered so rationally objective as to enter into the common fund of science accumulated for the body of the faithful as a whole.

Systematization begins, in truth, from the very definition of terms, a necessary preliminary to the construction of any certain conclusions. Different meanings given to the word Liberty, to the conception of causality, to the idea of humanity or to the part played by analogy will engender different "theologies". One will differ from another if it take as the keystone of its Christology the unity of the Person or the duality of natures— and so, in its ecclesiology, the transcendence of the mystery of the Church or its immanence in human history. Present-day controversies about Catholic Action are at bottom controlled by these somewhat ill-defined pre-suppositions. Again, a theology which sees the sacraments as primarily remedies for sin will differ from one which sees in them chiefly the means for promoting grace. Orthodoxy in the faith, perfectly preserved by both parties, cannot resolve these differences, but they go very deep into our minds and can have momentous effects. The most significant pointer to this distinction between faith and system is this—that the ministers of the Church, holding their mandate by succession from the apostles, have traditionally drawn a practical distinction between the teaching which they give, officially, as the true witnesses of the Word of God and the personal opinions which they offer in virtue of their own systems of theology. So far from impairing the obedience of the faithful in matters of faith and morals, this distinction guarantees the truth of the doctrines and the rightness of the conduct in question within the unity of the faith.

In our own time the "systems" have fallen into disrepute which is understandable in the circumstances but which has been a grave source of weakness. No doubt polemical excesses between rival schools led eventually to a neglect of the faith's main task and a diversion from the faith's main object. It was certainly disastrous that theological zeal in the eighteenth century devoted itself to the production of hundreds of folio volumes on the *de Auxiliis* controversy at a time when, outside the faith, a whole host of humane studies, based on political economy, were being brought to birth. Nor is there any doubt that, in reaction against the rationalism of the enlightenment and its sequel in the nineteenth century, men have come to perceive the limitations of reason when brought face to face with the Christian mystery and to realize the gulf separating religious experience from the categories of philosophy. From this point of view the renaissance of pastoral and dogmatic theology at Tübingen, the great work of Scheeben (d. 1888) and, moreover, the return to the writings and to the true spirit of the Fathers have done much to clear the air and to revive the sense of mystery in theological studies. This is something which system-building, if pursued for its own sake, tends to diminish but which the reading of the Gospels nourishes and fosters.

But while recognizing these risks and admitting past excesses we still maintain that theological systems are both necessary and true. Once you have admitted reason, with its triumphs and limitations, into this field at all, logic demands that you take this further, constructive step. Moreover truth itself, in its transcendence, invokes a multiplicity of points of view. We find this even in the disciplines of philosophy; all the more should we expect to find it when the radical inadequacy of our minds is faced with the revelation of God. Truth is unquestionably one, and a diversity of systems is a weakness; and for that reason even the most rigid system ought somehow to overstep its own boundaries, as it were—not by way of compromise with some rival system nor even in order to preserve charity in controversy but in the conviction that faith has a supreme simplicity and unity. In distinguishing the science from the systems we take our stand at the exact fulcrum where the theologian's discretion reveals itself, the precise cross-roads of his two convictions and his two enthusiasms: the primacy of the given revelation and the edifice of thought which he erects.

Besides, the worker in this field is still a believer and his work is still religious work, intelligibly religious. To make sense of the efficacy of the sacraments by a theory of instrumental causality is not an empty pastime. To seek to organize the theological data round the concept of Being is not gratuitous theorizing. Two distinct mentalities, two spirits are the fruits —or rather perhaps the roots—of these two modes of thought. It is good work, solid work, work in the service of truth. People who set it aside and nurse a general distrust of all systematization are like those people who declare that they will have nothing to do with politics. They *are* concerned with politics, willy-nilly, and concerned in the worst possible way, making decisions unconsciously, irrationally, uncritically.

It is not only the conceptual apparatus which differentiates one system from another but, more especially, as we said just now, an *original vision* which tends to create in the mind a livelier sensibility towards certain aspects of things, an inner logic to which the technical apparatus spontaneously bends itself, an attribution (sometimes unconscious) of priority to some part-truth passionately held. A "system" is therefore not a mere consequence resulting from the dialectic of thesis and conclusion; it is the product of a sort of condensation, distilled in the mind's profoundest depth. At certain cardinal points, on pain of reducing the inner tension of the system to a dialectic of *sic et non* (a phrase, by the way, which admirably expresses that tension), we must somehow attain to a kind of double intuition, an esoteric coherence—such, for example, as occurs at the heart of the problem of creation (sovereign independence of God: metaphysical value of reality) or in the conception of man (liberty of the human spirit: human involvement in the universe). This is something that goes beyond the reasoning intelligence. "It is esential to Thomism", says Maritain,[1] "that it demands a rigorous subordination of all that concerns technique and machinery to that which concerns the immanent activity and vital movement of intellection. It is not a 'system', an artifact. It is a living organism. The ligaments binding it together are living sinews, where each part only exists by virtue of the existence of the whole. The chief members here are not the initial members but rather the dominant members, the central members—and each, by implication, already contains the whole." The acid test of success is this: that the most rational parts of the system should discover their decisive light by returning to those original institutions, by "resolving" (as the Platonists say) the basic principles which have in reality been in constant if covert control throughout.

This is why, so far from feeling a sort of guilt-complex about the rigidity of a system, or being very liberal and accommodating towards different systems, we believe that the truth of reason and the truth of faith are better and more truly served by maintaining theological systems in their full integrity—while recognizing, of course, in all orthodoxy, the relativity of each system in regard to the absolute truth of faith.

Still more do we reject the attitude of those who, under the pretence of recognizing this relativity, plunge into eclecticism and see nothing in the rivalry of theological "schools" but a

[1] *The Degrees of Knowledge*, new trans. (London, Geoffrey Bles, and New York, Scribners, 1958).

rather peevish way of upholding a freedom of opinions which, by cancelling each other out, preserve the dogma which is superior to them. We believe in theological reasoning; eclecticism evades it. The relativity of systems is revealed precisely in their unequal value in respect of intelligibility, and therefore of truth—either because of ill-success in coordinating the given data, or because their structure is ill-organized, or because they start from material that is limited or ill-digested. It is the same with theological "errors", as well as with improbable opinions. The divine truth of faith is perhaps not compromised by the disqualification of a system, but it does not shine forth in human radiance save in such measure as the system which claims to express it renders possible.

THE VARIOUS THEOLOGICAL SYSTEMS

The whole history of Christian doctrine attests the plurality of theological systems. In rehearsing them we hope to illustrate the transcendence of the faith as well as the truth of these theologies.

The chief example (too much neglected, alas, because of a sort of tacit acquiescence in division, human and religious) arises from the spiritual geography of Christendom, the separation of east and west. After many centuries of history, and from a better understanding of the Greek Fathers, we now have a more lively sense of the divergence between their two theologies. We grieve to recognize herein one of the most deep-seated causes of the schism; but we may rejoice if, in the unity and orthodoxy of the faith, we have the wit to perceive herein two complementary endeavours to possess the mystery and to be possessed by the mystery—the one, whole and revealed truth. We know what tensions arose, this side of heresy, between a theology of the Trinity founded upon the plurality of persons, upon a direct faith in the Father, the Son and the Holy Ghost on the one hand, and on the other hand a systematization where the unity of God dominated a study of the relationships within the divine essence. Similar differences in their mental attitude affected men's approach to the central mystery of Christianity itself.

[Irenaeus, the Alexandrians and the eastern Doctors in general] considered the redemption of the world as one unique indivisible mystery, a single drama of God and Man, embracing all humanity and the whole of creation, in which the resurrection of the body and the life everlasting constitute the divine "catharsis". This conception stresses the deification which has already begun in the work of redemption; it is maintained to this day in the oriental Churches, notably in the very moving ceremony of their Easter vigil. In the west, contrariwise, before the restoration of the Easter vigil, the celebration of the mystery of Christ the Redeemer seemed often to centre upon the cross. This was viewed by some people as a one-sided distortion; but others saw in it an admirable liberation from neo-Platonist categories, a purer conformity with Scripture and a closer contact with the realities of human life—as if the wound in our created nature were never to be healed, as if we could never for one moment forget the infirmity of our present condition nor dream of the harmony of the world to come, as if St Paul had not seen the whole of creation drawn up into the glory of the risen Christ. It is a fact that, partly as a result of medieval theories about the nature of redemption and ransom but still more as a result of the pathos surrounding the commemoration of the Passion—in the veneration of the true Cross at Jerusalem and later in the medieval monasteries—the Cross came to dominate the picture, towering above the radiance of the empty sepulchre and appearing, here and there, to drive away remembrance of the glory.[2]

In this analysis one can see how liturgical forms, spiritual trends and scriptural emphases, working in the subsoil of theoretical controversy, penetrated the whole fabric of popular Christian piety. And at the same time one can foresee the rebound, the lasting effect this process would have on those same theoretical problems. The unitary and dynamic vision of

[2] F. Van der Meer, *St Augustin pasteur d'âmes* (Paris, 1955), II, p. 31.

the east goes forward to another plane, with a dualism of Nature and Grace, a division of theology into two parts in which "divinization" is superimposed upon a pre-existing nature, grace becomes an existent reality rather than a remedy or cure, our re-creation is brought about not by a *reformatio* raising man to a higher state than Adam's, but by a return to the state of paradise, to the ideal and truly "natural" condition of man, the starting-point of a cosmic progress rather than the scene of original sin, etc.

It is a fact that every time this oriental theology filters westward it is at once received with reserve, sometimes with hostility. Its cosmic and Christological optimism is rather shocking to the mind of the west, dominated as it is by the Augustinian view of the universe and of sinful humanity. Here is a single but twofold truth which the theologian finds it hard to maintain in perfect balance. The optimism of many currents of theology runs counter to a supernaturalist pessimism enshrined even in certain theological text-books.

In the west itself, in the course of its own historical development, two forms of thought have appeared successively— "monastic" theology, as it is called nowadays, and "scholastic" theology. The traditional division of history into Antiquity, Middle Ages and Renaissance is an over-simplification even in the cultural sphere, and when applied to the history of Christendom it has introduced a most pernicious division of values and caused deplorable confusion in the appreciation of theological trends. Of course, in so far as secular history enters into the sphere of religion, there was a "renaissance theology" in reaction against "medieval theology"; but this distinction, borrowed as an afterthought from a particular conception of European culture, obliterates a much more real distinction whose origin lies in religious attitudes themselves and the alterations which are normal to them. One of these theologies is rightly called "monastic" because the masters of it were for the most part monks and, more important, because it is linked to a particular attitude towards the world and the Christian household—of the Christian household *in* the world. But this monastic theology is of much wider scope than its name implies. We are not concerned with something which happened as a result of an historical coincidence and flourished in a circumscribed area which the Church in her development has outgrown. Here is no mere archaeological site from which certain objects can be excavated to show the continuity of tradition but which is otherwise a ruin quite useless to modern theology with its centuries of scholasticism and its contemporary problems. No; to speak of monastic theology as merely "prescholastic" is both false and offensive.

We have given a sufficiently high place to "scientific" theology and its scholastic techniques to entitle us now to accord a proper status and a permanent value to the theology called "monastic". It is not the least of the benefits conferred on us by Dom J. Leclercq (among many others) that he has drawn out, as it were, the monastic fund from the private estate of the scholars and proclaimed it credit-worthy.[3] The forthcoming celebration, at Bec, of the ninth centenary of St Anselm's becoming a monk (in 1060) will afford a happy opportunity to acclaim the relevance of his genius to the Church of the twentieth century, and to reaffirm the value, today, of a particular manner of contemplating God, of understanding his plan and his providence and how they operate in human souls and human history.[4]

We repeat here what we wrote about the masters of the famous Abbey of Jumièges and which we extend to all generations of monks—more especially those who, in the twelfth century, took cognizance of their originality at a time when a new theological method was being built:

> The value of this monastic theology has by no means been outmoded or outgrown, as a radical evolutionist might be dis-

---

[3] J. Leclercq, *L'amour des lettres et le désir de Dieu* (Paris, 1957).

[4] "Anselm, creator with Abelard of the scholastic method." This cliché, which expresses the connections and interchanges between two different theologies, is the result of historical and doctrinal confusions which we repudiate. The monks must not monopolize the genius of St Anselm.

posed to think and as some people in the days of Alexander of Jumièges were already beginning to think. Like the *Ordo monasticus* itself, it expresses values that are perennial, in the Church and in Man.

The presence of the written Scriptures, the absolute value of the faith as such and what it affords for silent adoration; the sense of mystery, which St Bernard rightly defends (apart from its excesses) against the attacks of Abelard; the scorn for dialectic when it becomes self-satisfied and self-sufficient, the superiority of wisdom (both in understanding and knowledge) over any science, even a sacred science; the impoverishment of the "theologian" when he becomes a mere professor—all these are always valid, and the monasteries, those *Scholae Christi*, bear necessary and lasting testimony to them. In them, moreover, human culture blossomed and spread, rooted in that healthy faith and in a spirit of humanism which, alas, the scholastic method was destined to lose. Jumièges, like other monastic centres, remains loyal to that tradition. And the name of William of Jumièges is enough to give the place of honour to his abbey in that historic awakening which remains one of the glories of twelfth-century monasticism—in spite of all the schoolmen who were destined, one day, to lose the sense of mystery and, along with it, the sense of history—the history of the earthly household of the kingdom of God.[5]

Within the major theological groups there were not lacking occasions and motives for a further multiplication of theologies. Some, like St Thomas, have taken an optimistic view of nature, of man and of reason, regarding them as belonging to divinity. Their motto was "grace does not suppress nature; it perfects it". Others, in the tradition of St Augustine—or rather by being more or less continually influenced by various followers of Augustine, from St Bernard to the author of the *Imitation*— saw rather the corruption of nature and the efficacy of grace (*Imitation of Christ*, Bk. 3, 54–5). These insist on the *absolute* character of grace, quite apart from its implantation in human souls and in temporal history. It was in this conflict, as is well

[5] See *Jumièges, Congrès du XIIIᵉ centenaire* (Rouen, 1955), p. 781.

known, that St Thomas's lot was cast, and there in the golden
age of scholasticism he played his hard and difficult rôle,
disconcerting his contemporaries not only by his Aristotelia-
nism but by the theological conclusions of his thought. We
know how, faced by passionate loyalties in a world of change
and growth, he had to submit to the most mortifying suspicions
and to condemnation by one of the highest doctrinal authorities.

Some, like the Antiochian Doctors of old, fix their eyes on
the duality of natures in Christ, and therefore in Christ's mystical body, the Church. The Jocist of today is fully aware of
Christ's humanity, and the priest of the *Mission de France* is
haunted by the reality of the incarnation and its temporal
"engagements". Others, like the Alexandrians, approach the
brink of a mystical and theocratic monophysitism.

Some have sought to integrate the humanistic values of the
renaissance and to reconcile liberty and grace; others deny
that human liberty and autonomy are in any way impaired by
the over-riding Providence of God. In ethics, one party relies
on the dictates of prudence, based on a rational judgement that
is centred on spiritual ends and practical experience; another
transfers moral decisions and the criteria of perfection to the
resolutions of the will and, in social matters, to obedience towards authority. There are those who, devoted to the supremacy
of the "inner life", think first of the salvation of individual
persons and trust that the reformation of human minds will
bring in its train the reformation of human society. Others,
preoccupied with the collective aspect and the priority of the
"common good", concentrate on forming societies—spiritual
and temporal—in which individuals may dwell, and these
therefore labour to reform the social structure. And so it goes
on. The story of theological schools of thought is played out
within the boundaries of theology itself. In order to appreciate
the strength, the limits and the criteria of theological knowledge
one must rise above controversies and disagreements.

We may add that at a time when the whole complex of
western civilization is challenged by the demographic and

political growth of other peoples, the fact that western Christendom has attained to certain assured truths should not blind us to the genius and achievements of other civilizations. We have good reason to hope that not only sanctity but theology also may gather fresh reinforcements for the understanding of the faith from the indigenous philosophies of other cultures—in India, the Far East and Africa. These are veins of precious metal, said Pius XI, which could bring a new radiance to the Gospel, not merely a sort of spiritual colonization. The Church, in this matter, possesses light and hope which astonish the politicians.

THE THOMIST SYSTEM

Should we then be indifferent to the quality and secondary values of theological systems? Granting that the faith itself transcends them, the Church has always upheld what may be called the liberty of the schools, provided that orthodoxy is preserved; and she forbids the theologians to cast doubt on the good faith of their colleagues because of divergences in their thought. Nevertheless within this regime, founded on the faith's transcendence, there has gradually grown up, in the west, a preference for the theology of one Doctor in particular. His canonization in 1323, fifty years after his death, was explicitly due to the quality of his teachings. From John XXII (who canonized him) onwards, the popes have delighted to honour the theology of St Thomas. In the critical period of the Reformation, at the Council of Trent, a reference to St Thomas carried authority. In the nineteenth century Leo XIII continually upheld him—although more for his efficacy in apologetics and philosophy than for the theological positions which he adopted. This authority is now ratified by the law of the Church where it is laid down, in the chapter on the training of the clergy (canon 1366), that they should be instructed "according to the method, the doctrine and the principles of the Angelic Doctor".

There are differences as to how the import and scope of this law should be interpreted and applied. The encyclical *Studiorum ducem* of Benedict XV (1920), although it confirms the rule, does introduce a formula which mitigates its rigour. Many papal pronouncements, too, have frankly commended other Doctors—Augustine, Anselm, Bonaventure, Francis de Sales, Bellarmine. But however that may be, there is no denying the privileged status of Thomism, the system of St Thomas Aquinas.

That the Church should express her preference is something which not only falls within the scope of her authority to teach; it must also affect our judgement of the religious truth of a system, and the exercise of such judgement is, as we have seen, our duty. There are various reasons why the Church should prefer the Thomist system. The first is, no doubt, that this system best assures the truth and the propagation of the faith in such a way as to minimize the "human element" which sometimes introduces opinions that are dangerous if not heretical. It also appears that, pedagogically speaking, the teaching of revealed truth, especially to young clergy whose task it is to transmit it, is best achieved by the system of the Angelic Doctor. In method and in content it gives to the expression of the faith a safe and opportune counterpoise of pure reason.

No doubt one needs to go further and consider that "content" itself. There can be no question of imposing the *opinions* of St Thomas as a substitute for the faith. But the Church's preference for Thomism is based upon the coherence of a system which, through centuries of flux in philosophy and religious experience, has proved the best adapted to keep the truths of religion in their right place—truths which may easily become distorted by their very attractiveness, whether in the passionate preaching of the Gospel or in the discovery of the powers of pure reason. The maintenance of a wise balance guarantees the breadth of his thought.

And therein lies the final reason for the Church's preference. Theological systems as such, by the very fact that they are systematic, tend to become narrow, in their principles and their intuitions. The system of St Thomas is the least "systematic", the most universal, the best adapted to take account of fresh discoveries—in the universe of grace and the universe of nature. *Noblesse* on such a scale *oblige*. History teaches many lessons in this sphere, and the Church has learned them.

CHAPTER VI

POSITIVE, SCHOLASTIC,
SPIRITUAL, PASTORAL

To the uninformed reader who opens a treatise on theology the arrangement of its chapters and the subdivisions of its subject-matter at first sight cannot fail to seem highly incongruous, even though each element retains its own proper value. After a regular appeal to various authorities we come upon an argument about formal logic; an historical inquiry interrupts a speculative discussion; mystical exaltation is superimposed upon rational criticism; casuistry sits sometimes alongside an archaeological explanation, sometimes beside some grandiose vision of the universe. What common denominator can we find in this jumble of facts and inferences?

This impression is reinforced when we notice that theology is divided and subdivided into more and more specialized sections, treated of in different and ill-assorted books, taught in independent lessons without a unifying curriculum. Two main sectors, exploited along utterly different lines, have nothing in common but their frontiers—the theology called "positive" and "scholastic" theology. The teacher of dogma has not the same methods as the teacher of moral theology, and it is not without some contention that they divide common material between them. Then, there are histories of doctrine, and histories of the spiritual life. An author will write a treatise of perfection in two parts—ascetical theology, mystical theology. Lately there has made its appearance a branch called pastoral theology, organized on new lines and with accredited teachers; but no agreement has yet been reached on its scope. Casuistic theology, which took shape three centuries ago, seems on the other hand to have fallen out of favour. What are we to make of these divisions of subject and method?

We must first of all admit that such a multiplication of methods and subjects within a single discipline is a natural result of its progress, as an increasingly searching analysis discerns differences of formal aspect within a whole which is materially one. This is a law governing all knowledge which applies naturally and properly to theology. No doubt some of the subdivisions mentioned above imply the more or less conscious adoption of certain attitudes towards nature or towards theological principles: the separation of ascetic from mystical theology presupposes a particular view of morality and grace; the pedagogical distinction between dogma and morals implies that the Thomist synthesis has been abandoned. Nevertheless specialization is valuable. "Positive" theology, for instance, investigates the faith's origins, and this has been useful not only, as at the critical period of the Reformation, in establishing the authenticity of the Church's teaching but also in deepening our knowledge of the documentary and nutritive character of the revelation itself. That one man should, according to his ability, make a specialized study of the history of spiritual doctrines, leaving to another the history of dogma, is something which in principle can only facilitate and improve the quality of the research itself. That pastoral theology should not be reduced to a set of corollaries annexed to various scholastic theses but should build up an autonomous function of its own is something which, in itself, can only make for progress.

At the present day, however, in theology as in other mental disciplines, one would like—without losing the benefits of specialization—to rediscover the inner unity of all true knowledge and to pay more attention to its synthetic coherence. At all events there are some subdivisions—resulting, no doubt, from the accidents of polemics or from presuppositions of doubtful validity rather than from the formal structure of the discipline in question—which need to be reconsidered. In truth, it is as well to establish the supreme rule of a science which, grafted upon the science of God, must always be turned towards unity; the law of an intelligence which, proceeding from faith in the Word of God, can never consent to receive the content of that Word in bits and pieces.

Theology is one, with a unity such as other branches of human knowledge can never pretend to. The history of philosophy bears witness that the greatest philosophers have regarded theoretical knowledge and practical knowledge as two quite separate domains, in practice irreducible and in principle governed by opposite methods. And each of us knows by living experience that the gulf between what we envisage and what we do is the tragic defect in human conduct. The theologian is not, in practice, exempted from this defect and, in principle, he recognizes a diversity of methods. Nevertheless he is for ever haunted by the unique "life-truth" which is the Faith, and therefore he strives with all his strength to resolve those differences, and he regards his knowledge as being in the highest degree both theoretical and practical. There may be differences of depth, differences of vocabulary—certain theologians have held, and still hold, that theology, being the science of salvation, is primarily a practical science; but the keystone of the whole building is unique: the divine science is such that in it the disjunction between thought and action no longer exists. However inaccessible it may be in practice, this ideal is always present at the very heart of all theological knowledge.

That is why certain features of religious instruction invite criticism—the divorce between *dogmatic* teaching and *moral* teaching, and, still more, that old schism, preserved in some catechisms—truths to be believed, commandments to be obeyed, sacraments to be received. This divorce belongs purely to the material plane and with its dull, inevitable weight may end by bringing falsehood into doctrine and hypocrisy into morals.

The subdivisions of moral theology seem to have suffered still more from presuppositions which are either clumsy or of doubtful validity, and in consequence the very name of *moral* theology has become debased, as if the science of practical duties were the second-rate semblance of a life which, in its perfection, derives from *spiritual* theology. Its ponderous vocabulary betrays the sickness into which both the teaching and the quality of theology can fall.

The distinction between "ascetic" and "mystical" theology arose from a similar sickness, and also originally from a particular conception of grace which found its highest states in extraordinary interventions by God himself. Recent controversies have more or less healed this vexatious schism, while admitting the benefits which a psychological distinction has brought to the analyses of spiritual phenomena.

"Pastoral" theology derives, within the unity of theological knowledge, from its *practical* character. It envisages action not only within the laws of a personal Christian life but within the theoretical and practical constants of a life lived in a community —in small communities (parishes, action groups, families, professions, etc.) and especially in the great community of the Church, the Body of Christ, established by apostolic succession, living in the world where she grows in the soil of secular reality. Having formerly given ground to individualism the theologians of today now appreciate with more lively clarity the sociological aspects of the faith, of its transmission, of brotherly love, of sacramental life. The growing socialization of whole sectors of human life make this revival necessary. The reawakening of pastoral theology, the foundation of special chairs in universities and seminaries, the publication of books on religious sociology, the establishment of definite zones of pastoral activity—all these are excellent signs of the revival of theology itself, which has always found truth and vigour when it has been the clear and well-knit expression of the Church in action. Pastoral theology is without doubt the most active member of the theological team at the present day. Yet it must never be cultivated apart. Empiricism has its limits which no fervour can conceal. It must still remain permeated by doctrine, understanding and contemplation.

The distinction between "positive" theology and "scholastic" theology is based on different principles and poses different problems. It arose, at least in its present-day form, as a result of controversies with Protestantism and from the need for a return to the living sources of the faith, for a precise inventory of its contents and for an intelligent grasp of the data of revelation in all its forms. Critical editions of ancient texts— of Scripture, the Fathers, spiritual writers—were an essential technical preliminary in the combat against renaissance scepticism and reformist excess. And so from the very beginning there arose a strange and deplorable animosity between these "positive" theologians and those of the scholastic tradition. The poisonous atmosphere engendered by this disease lingered on well into the twentieth century. The establishment of an "historical method" came into collision with a pseudo-dogmatism and the modernist heresy interrupted the sane and healthy search for a just appreciation of the relationship between the established truth of revelation and its doctrinal elaboration. Two opposite excesses, historicism and theologism, were the ill consequences of this schism between positive and speculative theology.

The crisis has now been overcome and the agreed diversities of method have been regulated not only by an exact appreciation of the needs of orthodoxy but by the reconciliation of faith and reason, of the facts of sacred history and the rational understanding of the revealed "economy".

Let a problem be properly set forth and its solution becomes obvious. Specialization of functions may require, and personal preferences and opportunities may demand, that a distinction be drawn between "positive" and "speculative", but the two are linked by the word "theology" which fixes and makes real their functional unity within the science of the Word of God. It is admitted, of course, that history and speculation are, in their methodology, incommensurable. One might accumulate a hoard of historical facts and of inferences based upon those facts, but the inferences would still remain external to the facts; speculation would not be history nor history speculation—and theology as a simple juxtaposition of the pair would not exist at all. But in truth theology does exist because it is greater than history and greater than scholastic speculation. Through faith theology hangs upon the revelation of God in the history of the sacred facts, the rational understanding of which enables us to take part in the divine plan and to partake of the divine knowledge.[1] History and speculation find their unity in the faith of the faithful, in the life of the apostolic society, the Church, and in the life of every believer who partakes of it. This is the traditional doctrine of St Thomas: the revealed truths, which are the bases of theology, must be grasped (positively and speculatively) where they are to be found revealed. It is by being so revealed, in faith, that they become the bases of theology. So we return to the first law, to the nature of theology as something that entirely hangs upon the Word of God. Because God speaks in human language, theology is intimately conjoined to the theandric mystery of that Word of God. *Verbum caro factum est.*

The final link in the unifying chain is this: theology is a "wisdom", in the ancient sense of the word. Though it has suffered some debasement in modern times, the word does retain a special quality and significance, especially in comparison with the word "science". A science holds no jot of mystery. It is a coherent system of rational operations which are immediately intelligible. But "wisdom" includes within itself the inner depths of spirituality and ineffable mystery; it can never become wholly objectified; and even the most thorough-going intellectualists attribute to its emotional profundity the original force of their own perceptions. St Augustine expressed not only

[1] We may pause to admire the wisdom of the Greek Fathers who distinguished between "Theologia" (science of God in himself) and "Economia" (science of God's plan in history).

his neo-Platonic psychology but also his conception of religious knowledge in terms of this dualism of science and wisdom: theology was for him a wisdom, not a science.

In the final analysis we can distinguish—though without opposing—two ways in which the wisdom of the faith develops. Either it is acquired doctrinally, by study and instruction, in the form of true propositions; or else it is the fine fruit of a lively desire and inclination, ripened by an emotional kinship with the object—the object both of knowledge and of love— even though opportunity for study may be lacking. A mother knows her child in this way, a way which quite transcends any academic study. In Christian doctrine this wisdom, where faith is concerned, is the effect of a gift of the Holy Spirit, and "theology" properly so called belongs to the former, the doctrinal, category. But woe to those who dissociate these two roads to the knowledge of God. They may arise from different principles and different disciplines, but they do not impair the essential unity of life and of grace.

Besides, even on its own level, theology is *wisdom*. Its task is to unite in a higher unity the various functions of theological "science"—from its technical equipment to its regulatory functions in the pastoral and ethical spheres. Though each sub-section be autonomous in respect of its own methods they must all work in the service of a single all-embracing vision which will always transcend the particular interests of the component parts. Thus the *wisdom* of theology gathers up and unifies many strands which are, humanly speaking, disparate— some of them eternal truths, some plunged in the temporal and contingent world, some the fruit of contemplation, some concerned with action—according to that division of functions which institutionally (and, alas, in practice too) distinguishes the "theologian" from the "apostle".

Now within the spiritual jurisdiction of the faith things temporal and things eternal are *not* any longer disparate objects: God and creature, hidden mystery or biblical history, eternal Word or Word made flesh, contemplative speculation or rules of conduct, sacramental symbolism or communion of saints, dialectical technique or loving contact—all, all alike spring from one same principle of knowledge, from one formal pattern of assent. The light of faith, at work scientifically, establishes one and the same field of intelligibility.

The same applies to the science of Scripture. From the earliest centuries the laws of biblical exegesis have been codified in a scientific form, and of this hermeneutic work nothing is lost, nothing need be lost. But despite the diversity of functions, especially in the literary and historical technicalities of exegesis, the wisdom of theology can still be nourished by scriptural meditation, for the Scriptures are a perennial source of both matter and light to which the loftiest speculation forever returns. The *doctrina sacra* in its unity (as we have said) extends from the shortest verse in Genesis to the most subtle inference of the Schools. Positive theology, speculative theology: but one unique wisdom.

It is true that this lofty vision—which we owe, in letter and spirit, to St Thomas—implies a particular conception of man, and of his understanding. In contrast to the majority of theologians, influenced by St Augustine, Thomas Aquinas denies that there are two "zones" of the spiritual life—one turned towards God, wholly spiritual, and therefore apt for purest contemplation in a timeless *wisdom*, while the other, bound to visible and tangible reality, rational in its operation, must be confined to *science* and to the temporal objects and methods of science. This dualism, wherein the spirit is bidden to shun the shadows and deceits of this world, as if the temporal order were by its nature a sort of stain upon the white radiance of truth, is an attitude which St Thomas rejects, down to its subtlest manifestations. As against this "eternism", whose doctrinal consequences may easily be guessed at, St Thomas holds that contemplation for an incarnate soul does not find its consummation in ecstasy, that wisdom (to resume our own vocabulary) is not to be attained by turning out of doors all the manifold sciences of this world.

This is the fundamental reason why theology in its various tasks, starting from its positive inquiry into the data of revelation and extending right up to the full scholastic discipline, can and should, in the light of the faith, exist *within* contemplation and within that wisdom which is a participation in the divine knowledge itself—of God and of the world alike.

CHAPTER VII

THEOLOGY AND CULTURE

In that very hour when Thomas Aquinas, professor in the university of Paris, was opposed by the majority of theologians and compromised by a condemnation of Aristotle on the ground that his methods were too rationalistic and his attitude too naturalistic, the Masters-of-Arts—that is, the whole teaching body in the faculties of letters and of science—rendered him public homage and, after his death, asked for the privilege of having his body for burial among them and of publishing the first edition of his works.

The incident is highly significant. In virtue of their doctrinal kinship with it, men of letters and of learning discerned the virtues of a theology which, as the science of God and therefore the apex of the hierarchy of sciences, guaranteed the rational validity of their own methods and disciplines and also brought to its highest level the principle of free research. Adherence to the teaching of St Thomas was their way of expressing both their Christian feelings and a defensive reflex against a theology, at that time the rival of Thomism, whose theocratic domination over the frontiers of both reason and faith they viewed with suspicion.

The problem of the relationship between theology and culture is in effect, on the plane of the intellectual organization of mental disciplines, a facet of the more general problem of the relationship between reason and faith. Several other volumes in this series are concerned with this general problem. Here, within the terms of our thesis and in line with our researches into the status of an organized theological knowledge, we are concerned with one final question: in order to play its proper part, not only in the life of this or that individual but also in the social cycle of a civilization, ought faith to develop in theological form? And how may theology then actively preside over the advance of human culture in a manner worthy of its sublime object?

Such a need will only be felt, of course, in a society where faith and grace are to be found in men's hearts—or at least in a collective body where they are socially present in some degree. In a universe which the Word of God had never entered, the relationship between man and divinity would be regulated by philosophy. So it was with the philosophy of the ancient world and with the civilization of the Hindus. In a Christian community, however, the private and public expression of the faith involves the need, among other needs, to build itself up (as we have said) in the form of a scientific discipline. It would be deplorable, it would be a real and grievous paradox if, in the face of worldly sciences rationally and adultly constructed, the faith were to remain in blinkers, the bright lamp of the Gospel behind shutters. Theology is a necessity for a Christian community. Psychologically, and in proportion to his personal culture, theology is a necessity for the humanely educated Christian. It is a necessity if only to satisfy a craving and hunger of the mind. It is distressing to find how often good Christians, very well educated in the worldly sense, have remained in the kindergarten so far as their faith is concerned. No ritual observance, no social and moral conformity, no pious obedience can compensate for this fatal impoverishment.

Turning to the social or collective side of the picture, a Church which did not accord to her theologians the right and the duty to bear organic witness to her faith in the cultural *milieu* wherein that faith was preached would be in a condition of mental anaemia. And by "cultural *milieu*" I mean not only the world of learning and philosophy but the economic and social world of the "small man". Remember that when, in the time of St Louis, the Parisian Masters-of-Arts held converse with Thomas Aquinas their common ground was the whole mental and moral environment of those days, down to quite humble relationships. Jean de Meung, author of the second part of the *Romaunt of the Rose*, who lived 200 yards from the university college of St James, adopted a naturalistic philosophy which the followers of St Thomas disapproved, and he was not always on friendly terms with them; yet he was given the honour of burial in their church. The leaders of the guilds and of the commoners were among their religious and intellectual clientèle and, in his conduct of the State, King Louis himself did not disdain theology. So at a time like this, when wide diffusion of culture and complexity of social institutions, even in the so-called under-developed countries, brings various pressures (both exalting and ambiguous pressures) to bear upon the spirits of men, the faith cannot maintain its consistency nor bear its witness unless theology—specialized, expert, highly intellectual theology—enables it to keep in step with the great scientific and cultural strides of humanity.

It is the Church's task, in her magisterial and pastoral capacity, to hold fast, to promote, to preach and to teach the Word of God whereof she is the guardian. Here the theologian, where orthodoxy, inner light and pastoral duty are concerned, is merely her loyal subject. But this loyalty, in engendering that "understanding of the faith" of which we have spoken above, confers on him a specific function whose framework, methods, freedom and range possess (in the light of faith and the communion of the faithful) a special status and a purpose which he alone can fulfil. Medieval Christianity, as we have seen, sets us an example which it would be childish to imitate but which it is more than ever important to follow. From the definition of theology which we have given it should be clear that there can be no question of taking refuge in the supernatural character of grace, no half-hearted rationalism which lacks confidence in the instincts of the human mind, no retreat into a blind obedience to authority. On the contrary, theology is an understanding which, in full continuity, spiritual and epistemological, with the Word of God, secures for faith a mental and cultural temper which is necessary not only to its efficacy but to its truth as well.

As for the precise position this theology may occupy in the world of culture, as for the manner in which this "wisdom" (to use the traditional term) should preside over the congress of the arts and sciences, and as for the part which the Christian should play in the intellectual life of the State and in the cultural activities of mankind, in these matters it is inevitable and natural that the diverse inspirations, systems and mentalities of different theological schools should have their own opinion and voice. Recent controversies on the relationship between evangelism and civilization are good evidence of the vitality and complexity of theology in the twentieth century. So let us imitate those great masters who, in the days of St Louis and St Thomas, set up before us the pattern of faithfulness, hard work and right decisions.

SELECT BIBLIOGRAPHY

BALTHASAR, Hans Urs von: *Science, Religion and Christianity*, London, Burns Oates, and Westminster, Md, Newman Press, 1958.

BONAVENTURE, St: *Breviloquium*, St Louis and London, Herder, 1946.

THOMAS AQUINAS, St: *Summa Theologica*, translated by Fathers of the English Dominican Province, three volumes, London, Burns Oates, and New York, Benziger, 1957.

HENRY, A. M., O.P.: *Theology Library*, four volumes, Chicago, Fides, and Cork, Mercier Press, 1956–8.

MARITAIN, Jacques: *The Degrees of Knowledge*, London, Bles, and New York, Charles Scribners, 1958.

SHEED, F. J.: *Theology and Sanity*, London and New York, Sheed and Ward, 1947.